The
ART
of
drawing
Closer
to
God

BELINDA É. SAMARI

WESTBOW
PRESS®
A DIVISION OF THOMAS NELSON
& ZONDERVAN

WestBow Press books may be ordered through booksellers or by contacting:

WestBow Press
A Division of Thomas Nelson & Zondervan
1663 Liberty Drive
Bloomington, IN 47403
www.westbowpress.com
1 (866) 928-1240

ISBN: 978-1-9736-0174-6 (sc)
ISBN: 978-1-9736-0175-3 (hc)
ISBN: 978-1-9736-0173-9 (e)

Library of Congress Control Number: 2017914189

Print information available on the last page.

WestBow Press rev. date: 03/05/2020

All of you who are in search of a personal God,
all of you who long to hear Him speak,
all of you who want an experience you will not forget,
this book is for you.

Dedicated to
the Holy One of Israel —
for having first written this on my heart,
then enabling me to write it on paper.

ACKNOWLEDGMENTS

This book has been in the making for *years*. What you hold in your hands is the result of many different people each putting their hands to join mine on the potter's wheel to make this what it is. I am indebted to these wonderful people: **Clara Cherry** and **Nin Clark** for reading this in the early days. **Dina Grohmann**, for your enthusiastic reading and support of this in its infancy. **Kärt Lazić** for wholeheartedly plunging into this manuscript, for your insightful understanding of the artistic and for sharing a wavelength with me. **Tihomir Lazić** for being a friend, an ally and a witness to this entire process, particularly for being instrumental in aiding me articulate my RH in LH language in the early days. **Chris McManus** for generously offering your psychological expertise and crucial feedback on the bit about the hemispheres, helping me ensure I had them wired properly (any remaining errors are my own). **Marco Mesa-Frias**, for bringing your LH to the early afts and enabling me to learn from you. **Zorica Nenadović**, for your nuanced understanding of spirituality and for making me realise I am a European thinker. **Melita Pujić Pažitka** for always being supportive of my creative endeavours and for your feedback when this was still hatching. **Zorica Samardzija** (Mum) it is to you that I owe my love of stories, storytelling, and a life with God, and **Jack Samardzija** (Dad), it is because of you that I so enjoy analysis, writing and research. Both of you put together are 'heart' and 'head' at their best. **Michael Samardzija**, cousin *par excellence*, your practical advice and guidance in the embryonic stages of this project were invaluable. **Herta Von Stiegel**, for your vital encouragement and practical perspective on this project. **Goran Stojanović** (Gogi), you saw this unfold over the years, and I am grateful for your support. **Laurence Turner** for graciously carving out time in your busy schedule to share your Hebrew Bible expertise and keen eye for detail. I am so deeply grateful for that and for your affirmation of this project. Finally, while not directly involved with this book, I would like to acknowledge my friends and colleagues **Lily Kahn** and **Willem Smelik** who played a memorable role in my love affair with Biblical Hebrew. To you all – an immense and profound *thank you.*

INTRODUCTION

"…[God], I get all muddled up… You seem to get lost (I lose You) in the noise and hubbub of the mundane and repetitive actions we call life and I lose my grip. My stability wavers, my confidence wanes and my solid foundation feels like it's dissolving beneath my very two feet. Stunned, I stand, paralysed, helpless and watch it all crumble to the ground. I wonder how I could ever find You again in such a mess. I know You're there. You're waiting for me to find You… **_I want to find You_**. *More than anything else. I want to learn and relearn how to find You, and keep close to You, even when the noise levels rise and the world around me begins to spin. Reach out Your hand and I'll reach mine out, and they'll meet…"*

*   *   *

Suddenly it hits you like a ton of bricks. You are told you have been let go and in a strange way your last day at work seems like the last day of your life… Your home and that for which you have worked for years is swept away one night in a flood… You discover your child is a drug addict and wonder how this happened to your family… Your marriage is falling apart and you cannot seem to stop the tower from toppling over… Your best friend eventually loses a long and painful battle with cancer… Sound familiar?

Whatever the scenario, of which I have named only a few, when we find ourselves in situations like these the experience is similar for us all: shock, fear, unspeakable pain, confusion, loneliness, helplessness, sadness, loss… A million questions poking and prodding: how did this happen? Why did it happen? Where did it all go wrong? What do I do now? Where do I go from here?

In an instant your whole world seems different, it is as though a game is being played and suddenly the referee blows the whistle and announces the rules have changed. 'But I don't know these rules', you might say, 'I have never played by them before. How do I learn them and what are they anyway?' Yet it seems that with another whistle blow the game resumes and everything continues on as usual, leaving you stunned and confused, wondering how you will find your footing in this new game in which you find yourself...

That was me, through and through, as seen in that excerpt from my journal you just read. I was so thrown by the whistle blowing, the new rules and the chaos of it all, I did not know up from down. Part of me was running on the field like a madwoman trying to keep up and catch on, and the other part of me just stood there, feet glued to the ground.

Where I start my story finds me deeply confused, my entire world had been smashed to bits and I did not know how to rebuild it. I lacked the tools, the knowledge of where to even begin. Even though it had been some time since that 'blow of the whistle', I was still struggling to find my footing and I desperately needed God. Sure, I had looked for Him before and had longed for Him to change my life. I prayed, I reflected on Bible passages, I tried to listen for His voice, I did everything I knew in order to connect more deeply with Him. And I cannot say I had never heard Him speak to me up until that point, but it had been faint, sporadic and I longed for something more obvious and concrete. I knew God was close, I knew He had not left me alone but so many times it seemed that He was distant and I was stuck in a haze of thoughts, longings and questions. Nothing seemed to be happening and I was getting discouraged. I wanted to hear Him, loud and clear. I needed Him to break through the confusion and darkness that surrounded me.

Against the backdrop of this mess I embarked on a journey. Not long after having bought a ticket from London to Sharm El Sheikh, I found myself on the Sinai Peninsula in Egypt and the moment was coming close - the moment when I was to begin climbing Mt. Sinai. This was not a tourist trip, this was not just a climb. This was for a need, my need of God, of His closeness and of His revelation to me. The Israelites had been there long before I had and had heard God speak. They had seen Him in the cloud and they had heard His voice in the thunder. They had received His words for them, words to live by, to follow, to help and to nourish, words of eternal value. What they did with those words is not the issue here. The fact remains: God had spoken and things had changed. A bond had been formed and sealed, a covenant, a sacred pledge to faithfulness had been reiterated in writing. Centuries later, here I was, waiting for my own experience, for my own thundercloud and my own tablet of stone. I wanted

God to so clearly and obviously reveal Himself to me, that I would never have doubts about whether or not He had. All those previous times I had sensed Him were subtle and quiet and I was not complaining. But at this point I needed loud and thunderous, I needed the *unmistakable presence* of the Almighty Himself. I longed for a Saviour and guidance that would make it clear what was best for me. I wanted to walk in those words, in that truth and for it to make a difference. I believed that in order for this to happen, an encounter was necessary – I needed to show up just as much as He did. I was ready to give everything of myself to make this possible; I trusted He would do the same. So with this in my heart, in the very depths of my soul, I ventured off onto this rugged mountain, into rough terrain, and sought to find God. But not just find Him – *experience* Him.

*   *   *

This book endeavours to combine creative methods to employ when exploring Biblical texts and themes with the aim of drawing closer to God and making the reading of the Bible a fuller experience. By and large, the ideas explored on the following pages can be divided into two larger sections.

As I briefly mentioned already, I begin by sharing my experience of climbing Mt. Sinai. This part of the book focuses on personal experience and the deep insight that can often come in unexpected moments and unexpected ways. The particular emphasis of this section is the way the human brain functions, the ways in which we expect to 'hear' from God and how we experience Him. Here you will find certain scientific underpinnings for creativity and different modes of expression and experience that will be followed by the more practical part of the book.

If you choose to embark on this journey, the second section will move you through Biblical texts one at a time, one a day, that centre upon a specific theme. These texts are accompanied by creative exercises designed to enable you to engage the text more meaningfully and personally, to help develop a fuller, holistic approach to the textual experience. The general aim is to bring greater flexibility to the way you think and to offer you a chance to re-wire established patterns of thinking and doing that are useful but limiting.

I am a psychologist with a specialisation in Expressive Arts Therapy, along with an MA in Hebrew and Jewish Studies and I am currently studying toward a doctorate in ancient Greek philosophy. I am also a musician and a composer and in a nutshell, all my work is thoroughly rooted in creativity. Though this is not an academic book you will notice that it is somewhat scholarly in that I have used footnotes – this is so you can follow up on whatever aspects of this book that interest you, and I have purposely kept them as footnotes rather than endnotes, because I personally find it disruptive having to flip backwards and forwards while I read! The reason why I have written this book is not only because the subject matter became personally relevant to me many years ago, but because over the years whilst working with people in all sorts of settings, I have noticed a great need for more clarity on how we experience God. In addition to that, I have also found that that clarity is largely dependent on our assumptions regarding the Biblical text, what it is and how we are to interact with it; hence this book.

That said, this book is not a magical formula for a certain type of experience of God, nor is it a theological or scientific manual of sorts. Essentially, I am offering these moments of my story to you as a fellow traveller in life, as one who struggles and triumphs, one who faces giant hurdles to overcome. In my experience the more we connect and exchange with each other the more we can be encouraged, and the more hope and strength we can find for our journey. So what I am bringing to the table in my desire to do just that are these few details of my own story in the hope that you will find something in it for yourself, something to hold on to even after you have read the very last page of this book.

The last thing that must be said before I proceed is that we all harbour preconceived notions of what it means to hear God, experience Him, to know His will for our lives. We look for God and when we do not seem to find Him, we wonder why. As I mentioned I had heard God speak to me before and He was no stranger to me. But I could not help but wonder if, when He had been speaking, I had been deaf to what He had been saying, with my mind and heart elsewhere. Perhaps I had not been thorough enough, and so I had failed to hear. Maybe

I had believed He was not speaking at all. This climb was about to change that. This climb would change things in a way I could never have anticipated or foreseen; its after-effect would be deep and its consequences profound.

Now, if you will, come with me, back to that night, as I waited for my encounter with the mountain.

*   *   *

BEFORE THE CLIMB

22:00 – 01:00

Yawn, stretch, glance at watch. 21:47. Sitting in the hotel lobby waiting for the bus to arrive. I did not know whether I was more sleepy or excited. I looked around at those who were waiting with me – Germans, French, Americans, mostly middle-aged friends or couples who had decided to make this journey together. I was doing this alone and somehow it seemed befitting – this was a personal quest and though I was not unfriendly, I actually enjoyed not having to chat or socialise. I closed my eyes and leaned my head back onto the sofa hoping to shut out some of the noise. The bus came half an hour late and, frankly, I was not surprised; we eventually piled in and began our two-and-a-half-hour drive to the Sinai desert. I was sitting by the window staring out at the sky. Velvet black, sprinkled with an ocean of stars and they shone on the barren desert below. I gazed at it tirelessly and could not help but smile at the mere thought of where I was going and what I was about to do. Most of my co-passengers were trying to catch up on some sleep, clever idea, and though I would have liked to have done the same, I could not, I was as excited as a child in a candy shop.

Interrupting the lulling rhythm of the drive, the bus was slowing down as I glanced about me to see what was happening. As we came to a halt I was blinded by lights and turned my head away as I squinted. We had come to a gas station, our one and only stop before reaching the mountain. Lavatory breaks were needed as we were to begin climbing shortly and there would be no such facilities till we reached the top. Yawning, my fatigue steadily seeped in through the cracks of my excitement and part of me wanted to succumb to the lure of sleep. Not having slept nearly enough the few nights leading up to this (mosquitoes), I felt like a pair of shoes that had been washed in the machine, tumbled around and drained when the cycle finally stopped. Not only was I increasingly sleepy, but now my stomach was growling too. The hotel food had gotten painfully dull seeing as the buffet offered the Same. Thing. Every. Day. (often the curse of the vegans and vegetarians) so I had not eaten the usual mountain of food to which I was accustomed. All in all, I was not at my fittest but I am not recounting this as a means of justification, merely as a glimpse into my state of being at the time. I thought to myself: I guess that is how life is, when great things happen, not everything in the outside world is perfectly lined up to match those experiences. That is to say, even though I was tired and hungry, it did not mean that something wonderful could not happen.

There were about thirty to forty of us in our bus and we were now called the 'Abdu' group. What we soon discovered was that there were several parties of our size, all geared up and ready to climb the same mountain. Each group had a name and this was necessary. Our group had two guides, Magda, a friendly Egyptian man from the tourist agency and Abdu (hence the name), a local Bedouin; the unspoken rule is that Bedouin guides are compulsory because of the dangerous terrain that is familiar territory to them.

There I stood, at the foot of Mt Sinai. Its enormous scale could not even be roughly estimated in the thick darkness that engulfed me. At the time I did not know it but a steeply inclined 2, 285 m (7,497 ft) that seemed to dissolve into infinity was piled high between me and the summit of the mountain. I took a deep breath; the night air was cold and fresh, cooler than expected as I zipped up my lightweight sweater. The stars were breath-taking, the Orion constellation fully visible and even the Milky Way. Looking up at them it seemed that were I to raise my hand, I would brush them with my fingertips. I still could not help smiling.

I made my final preparations as did the rest of my group. I retied my shoelaces, strapped my camera securely on my back and tied my hair up. I was ready to go. I felt as though I was doing something important, a marker worth noting in my life. The groups began to climb one after the other and we tried to do this in as orderly a fashion as possible. We were ants on a hill, a really big hill.

THE CLIMB

01:30-4:30

With a flashlight in one hand and a bottle of water in the other, I began my ascent. I had the extra weight of my camera bag on my back but did not really have a choice. The Canon SLR had a heavy body and an even heavier lens. Whatever was up there, however it looked, it had to be recorded and I was prepared to suffer for that. Little did I know just how much I would suffer for the next eight hours.

It is important to point out that, regarding the previously mentioned preconceived notions of God speaking to us, I had a rough picture in my mind of what the experience would be like. I knew it was not going to be an easy climb, I expected to break out in a sweat and get a little roughed up, so to speak, but I also thought that since this was to be a spiritual quest, I could listen to some spiritual music on my iPod on the journey up. I thought this would be a good way to connect to God while I was climbing this rugged beauty.

I began walking at a moderate pace feeling quite energised despite the fact that midnight had long passed. I looked around me and all my group companions also seemed to have bundles of energy that propelled them forward. Some whizzed past me with incredible speed and to my dismay they were those who I had seen putting out their cigarette butts just moments ago! Smokers overtaking me? Come on, I was a vegetarian! A non-smoking, healthy-living vegetarian and they were overtaking me! I have to admit, it made me laugh. Yes I know, being a vegetarian does not automatically make me fitter than the rest of the bunch, but still it amused me. We all briskly attacked the base of this gigantic creature but as we neared the first stopping point (a little wooden shack resembling a bus stop), we were all quite out of breath. I dared not think how much more ground there was to cover.

As I continued on my path a few things became clear. The energetic huffing and puffing of my fellow climbers was fading and gradually reduced to almost a whisper, the energy now simmering compared to earlier on. While they had chatted animatedly at the beginning of the climb, now they pushed on in silence. All of us had retreated into our inner worlds and were battling our way up. I became aware that I had only my little flashlight to light my path, so my eyes were constantly strained. I had to be vigilant about where I was stepping; the uneven terrain required care and complete concentration if I was to do this well. Soon I could hear only the sound of my own breath – inhale, exhale, inhale, exhale. There was no iPod in my ears and I realised there would be none at all. That notion had crumbled a few hundred steps back. At this point the thought of music in my ears seemed more like a nuisance, a distraction and not something I wanted to add to this increasing concoction of effort and concentration. I had no time to gaze at the stars and admire their beauty. I had no time to stop and rest whenever I felt like it. I had already, it seemed, fallen to the back of my group. Every so often our Bedouin guide would call out 'Abdu!' and that would be a sign for me, a way for me to know the approximate location of my guide and my group in that dense darkness. It was slightly odd, being out in the vast, open space of the desert and yet slightly crowded by enthusiastic climbers, some scurrying along past me. They were invisible individuals whose faces I could not make out in the darkness and yet whose presence was palpable. Even the mountain was mysteriously accessible yet elusive; it was tangible, firm beneath my feet yet completely veiled in a consuming darkness that was both unnerving and exhilarating.

Silence. Breathing. Sweat. Strained eyes. This was no picnic, it was not a leisurely stroll and my activities were reduced to a very few – 'always keep your eyes on the path, find the right place to put your feet, keep breathing evenly'. That is it. There was no spiritual fanfare, no glorious revelation nor a thunderous voice speaking words of wisdom to me. (For that matter, there was no still, small voice either.) No, this was hard work.

This was a trek on rough ground in conditions of limited visibility. Since I was sweating a lot, when I did stop to rest briefly, I felt the cold wind blow and I began to shiver. So I was tired when I climbed and cold when I rested! Marvellous. The climb was intense and continuous. I had no time to stop and sip some of my water, I had to do it whilst climbing for fear of falling even further behind. To make matters worse I would occasionally trip up on the feet of the camels lying on the side of the path, belonging to the native Bedouins who would offer to take me up two thirds of the way for only ten euro. That is all it would cost me for rest, for comfort – ten euro for the easy way out. But you see, before I had even begun to climb I had decided that was not going to be an option. Not because it was immoral in any sense to accept a camel ride, but because I wanted to climb this mountain on foot, feel it with every bead of sweat, every step of my aching feet. I wanted this to be the real deal. Having said that, it was incredibly tempting to pay and ride. Oh, it was, it most certainly was. As I passed the camels and their handlers on my path, their silhouettes vaguely discernable beneath the starry skies, they whispered of their offer, nudged and persisted. But I resolutely kept repeating '*La, shukran*, no, thank you'. Inside my head though, was another story.

Because things had quieted down and the crowd had dissipated, I was able to hear my own thoughts most distinctly. Perhaps for the first time, I could discern my own inner voice and thoughts with an uncanny clarity. This in itself was remarkable to notice, but what was even more astonishing was when I noticed what these conversations were about. As I passed the Bedouins and politely declined their offers, this is how the conversation sounded:

'Why don't you just do it? Why don't you just pay and ride, in comfort, get some rest? You need it. You're exhausted and you're not even half way there!'

'No, I don't want to. I can do this. Obviously I'm tired but I knew that would happen. I can do this.'

'No you can't.'

'You're right, I can't. What on earth *am I doing? Oh no no no wait! Yes I can! I* can *do this. Besides, I decided I wasn't going to ride. If I do, it'll be like copping out, like cheating somehow.'*

'It's not cheating; this isn't breaking a commandment or anything. It's a way to help you!'

'I know it is; but still, it's an easy solution and I want to go all the way with this, no matter what. I promised I would do everything from my side. I have to try; I have to go all the way.'

So as my perspiring body ached and inwardly groaned, my inner being raged with heated debate, and believe me, this wore me out more than the actual climbing did. This was not a one-off affair; this conversation lasted the *entire* climb, *the whole time.*

It was a tumultuous, fully-fledged battle and I had not seen it coming. I felt unprepared to face myself – the opposing views, the challenges and alternatives placed before me. When contemplating this climb I had only considered the physical aspect, but life is never just physical. It is always mental, emotional and spiritual as well, whether we are aware of it or not. Had I stuck my iPod in my ears as I had initially intended to, I would not have been able to hear this dialogue within (nor the guide's voice for that matter), I would have been unable to discern this element in the story. I would have focused on the physical battle, which was tough enough on its own, but that would not have been the whole story; there was more to it than that. Sometimes I notice this tendency in other areas of my life as well. I am tempted to focus on the visible, the immediate and the physical and thereby sideline vital aspects of my story. By focusing only on one element, I fail to see how they all fit together, how they interact and impact me.

I was a relentless Sisyphus, we all were, pushing ourselves up the mountain, only to roll down again a few hours later. By the time I had reached what I believed was the halfway mark, I was so exhausted, so weak, I thought I would never make it to the top. The meagre food servings of that day were taking their toll on me and my energy was draining, fast. When I stopped to rest, my legs shook like a leaf. Weighed down by my camera bag, my back ached. I longed for a bed, warmth, sleep and proper rest. But it was not to come, not for a long while yet. I had doubts about how I would reach the top. Even with all my goodwill and determination, I could not imagine how it would happen. Battling with uncertainty about my own capabilities, I pushed my willpower to the forefront of my mind and carried on. As I began to walk again, the conversation continued and seemed more audible than ever.

> *'You'll never get to the top, you're a failure.'*
> *'Yes I will, no I'm not.'*
> *'You are; you're weak and too tired to even think. Look at you... you think you'll make it to the top? No way!'*
> *'No! Stop saying that! I'm not giving up... I'm going to do this, whatever it takes. Even if I collapse on this mountain, I am __not__ giving up!'*

'I don't even know why I'm doing this. What am I trying to prove anyway? I should give up now and at least get some rest; it'll all be over then.'

'No! What am I saying?! I know this isn't about proving anything, but I'm going to do this and nothing will stop me. Oh my goodness, this is so exhausting!'

'Just look at yourself… you can barely stand on your own two feet. You're already wasted and you're nowhere near the top. Just stop now. It's so easy. Look to the side of the path. There, you can sit on that rock. It's so easy, just go over, and plop down on it, give in to it, you know you want to. Who are you doing this for anyway? It's not like you're going to get a prize or anything. This won't matter to anyone. No one even knows what you're going through. This isn't as important as you think it is, so come on, just give up!'

If it was not about one thing, it was about another. Sometimes this voice of my thoughts was seductive and gentle, other times it was outright aggressive. Crashing down on me like falling Domino came the reasons why I should stop and quit, throwing it all down the drain – my goal, my hope, my pilgrimage. I may have been climbing this mountain but I was wrestling with another – an oppressive mountain of objections to my search; a horde of logical and very rational reasons that ruthlessly pursued me, hunting me down as I struggled to escape them. Like starved predators they preyed on me, hoping to wear me out to the point of breaking down and giving in to my inevitable end.

To anyone else these thoughts might not have meant a lot, the decision to stop or continue might not have borne such great significance. For anyone else this might have been just another activity, another climb among many. But for me, at that point in time, this was the pivotal point upon which everything rested. This climb was about meeting God in a special way, and climbing, this way, rejecting camels, was my way of showing how much this mattered to me (how much *He* mattered to me). This was not about self-flagellation of any kind in order to obtain favour from above, but rather about wanting to immerse myself in this process as much as possible. My desire was profound, not half-hearted in the least and I hoped my climb reflected that. This was a quest fuelled by a deep hunger for something more. *This was not just a climb.*

The torment was disquietingly real yet abstract, felt but not seen. It was incredibly powerful and called out to me, the lone, vulnerable prey in so many ways. It was a strong call. It was a strong, unrelenting call to give up. Ultimately, for me in that situation, it was a call to *give up on God*. To give up on experiencing Him, to give up on hearing Him speak, to abandon going through with the expedition and go with what was easier, what was immediate and right in front of my eyes. Sitting on a rock and giving up would be easy, effortless. Believing and pushing forward to the top of a mountain I could not even see, that was much, much more difficult. I had no idea how far I still had to go. The part of the journey still ahead would require all of me – physically, mentally, emotionally and spiritually. I would either make it to the top or I would not – there was no other option. It was literally all or nothing.

I was scraping the bottom of my metaphorical jar for the last remains of my energy. With each step the dream of getting to the top grew dimmer. Apart from our Bedouin guide Abdu, our other friendly guide Magda had tried to keep an eye on me, noticing that I was alone. He made sure I was near the group, even if I was at the tail end of it. Now they were a long way ahead; only he had stayed behind to wait for me. He climbs this mountain at least twice a week, sometimes three times. To see him panting and out of breath was a small consolation, but it also told me that he could not carry me up there; I still had to do this on my own. He offered me his arm and I leaned on it and dragged my feet, putting one in front of the other, doing my utmost to manage the raging conversations inside and focus on literally taking one step at a time. If I so much as allowed my mind to wander to the top, the final destination, thoughts of despair flooded in faster than I could keep them out.

Now we were no longer even stopping at the designated rest areas. We passed them by, hurrying to get to the top. Why? Because we were supposed to be at the summit in time for sunrise, apparently a marvellous experience. I believed it would be, but would I get there in time? I kept tripping up and felt awfully feeble. The guide suggested I rest just a little and I did not protest. Had I not sat down for a minute or two I would have collapsed. First he tried to make polite conversation but soon realised I was too weak and told me to save my strength, that I would need it. Oh great! If I was yet to need it, how far off was this mountain peak?! We carried on, he already ahead of me, me trailing behind and fighting for every step. I had just rested for a moment or two and already I was so faint after barely a minute of moving on again that I was on the verge of losing hope.

Every time I slipped, his headlight whipped around so he could see if I was all right, till at one point he grabbed my arm and held me up as we then walked together. We climbed that way for what seemed to be an eternity. Then we finally reached the last stop before the next 750 'steps'. I sat down, completely crushed, sparingly sipping water and trying to stay warm. With the cold wind whipping my tired body, I was afraid of getting ill. On second thought, even that would be acceptable as long as I made it to the top; that was all that mattered.

At that point I lost Magda and I could not find him anywhere so I continued alone. My group had all but disappeared. There were others around me, from different parties and, to my dismay, it was at this point that people stopped climbing *en masse*. I did not even realise just how frail I was until I began to climb these 'steps'. They are known as 'the steps of penitence' though in actuality they are large boulders of stone, etched into the mountain. There are 750 of these 'steps' before one reaches the summit. I then realised and overheard that most people stop at this point because those steps are the most strenuous part of the entire climb. For those who ride on camels, this is their stop; the camels can go no further.

The steps form a very steep, narrow and difficult path up to the summit. I could feel the exhaustion pushing me to my very limits, inside and out. To bear on me even more heavily was the sight of masses of people just sitting down, stopping and ending their journey there. All around me, people giving up! This is not 'wrong', as I mentioned; making such a decision undermines no moral principle. But for me the implications were colossal. I needed support, encouragement, cheering! Where was all of that? I did *not* need this – a vivid example of what it means to choose comfort and surrender. I shoved negative thoughts aside and began to tackle the steps, one by one. They were giants to me, almost insurmountable obstacles followed one by another. These 'steps' were discouraging me from getting to my goal, yet at the same time fortifying my will to reach it. With each step I was a little higher, a little closer to the top. I gave it my all, I really did. I had to stop and rest roughly every two steps because I was so exhausted. Even when I did rest, I did not allow myself to rest for very long because each time I stopped it was harder to get up and get going again. Those who had been with me on this narrow path – people who had climbed the last two, or five steps with me – were no longer there. I looked back only to see them relinquishing and going in the opposite direction. Witnessing others forfeit harshly yanked on my own mental reigns and made it extremely difficult for me to continue. Thoughts of discouragement swarmed through my frazzled mind, the lure of renouncing my pursuit attracting them like a moth to a flame. To resist and subdue them was almost impossible. I cannot stress enough the fact that this was more challenging than the actual pain in my body. Without a doubt it was more powerful than my physical exhaustion. I did my best to refocus my thoughts every time I was tempted to give up and lose hope. I was so close! I *had* to make it, I just *had* to. Failure was not an option. At this point even my attempts to breathe evenly did not help. All along the way each of us had it hard, each in his or her own way; we all climbed in silence, lost in our own worlds as our bodies and minds ploughed forward.

I stopped to rest along this path of steps and I was struggling to the point of disbelief. In my journal in which I recorded all of this the day after the climb, I wrote that even then, I could not find the words with which to convey just how indescribably worn-out I had felt. I felt like an old rag ready for the rubbish heap. I pressed on but after a few steps I faltered. Again. It was then that I heard the voice of a Bedouin, a boy who offered to help. (When I say 'boy' I am guessing he was perhaps 19 or 20 years old.) I said '*La, shukran*'. I thought to myself, 'I'm not going to accept help from a complete stranger who appears to me out of the darkness, whose face I cannot even see. As if I am going to take him by the hand now and let him lead me!' I could do this on my own. A few steps onward I fell and I heard his voice again, offering help. This time I thought, 'What do I have to lose? He is only offering help, not his hand in marriage.' So I accepted! I chose to trust and rely on him and on his strength to get us both there. He walked at my pace and did not mind when I said I needed to rest again. (He spoke almost no English but collapsing in front of him clearly communicated the need for urgent 'rest'.) As I sat, breathing heavily, our guide Magda found me and wondered where he had lost me. He said he would go on with me so I thanked the young Bedouin and he vanished into the darkness from which he had emerged. Magda and I continued. He was my strength, he pressed on and supported me and at this point, he did most of the work. I did the minimum because that was all I could do, I was at my very lowest and it felt as though I would die (or at least collapse and fall asleep, or freeze or something quite dramatic like that). Here and there I would ask Magda how much further there was to the top, how much more of the trek was left to cover. He would always say, 'Don't worry; just keep going'. With a metaphorical eye-roll, I knew that meant there was plenty more to suffer otherwise he would have said something more encouraging! But at last when I asked one time, pointing he said, 'Up there, that's it.' I looked up and saw what appeared to be another resting station. With a faint but renewed vigour in my heart, I staggered up the remaining 'steps'. I reached the top of Mt. Sinai.

4:30-5:30

I could not believe it. There at the summit, still hemmed in by the spacious darkness, I leaned my hands on my shaking knees and just breathed, the cold air puncturing my lungs. Deep inside I was smiling; oh the relief of knowing it was over! I was stunned, amazed, drenched in fatigue but amazed nonetheless. I had given every atom of my energy, the very sap of my being to reach the top and I had done it. I was a wreck but I had made it. That realisation was yet to fully sink in.

The pre-dawn sky as though infused with jet-black ink, still concealed the sun in its veiled embrace; it would not show its face for another hour or so. I shuffled through the small crowd into one of the wooden huts there on the mountaintop. Ducking, I passed through the doorway and stepped inside, immediately hugged by the warmth. Lining the walls were benches covered with blankets and snacks and drinks were being sold - a small recompense for a tremendous effort. The tiny shack was full to the brim of us weary but triumphant travellers. This was also the first time I had seen some of my companions' faces. Chatter, excitement, anticipation, fatigue, exhaustion, all were squished inside the hut. I found a free space and squeezed in among them. I took a few bites of a snack bar for some energy and a few sips of *karkadé* tea to warm me up. Huddled up with the others and cradling my tea in my frozen hands, I fell asleep within seconds.

5:30-6:00

I was roused from what felt like the blink of an eye but was actually roughly half an hour of deep sleep. There was commotion all around me as the sun was announcing its majestic appearance and people were spilling through the tiny cabin door out into the open space. This was the climax, the moment we had all been waiting for. Rubbing my eyes in an attempt to wake up, to be honest there was a part of me that thought, *'Who cares about the sunrise? I was finally getting some sleep, just leave me here, I'll be fine. You go ahead and watch the sunrise and come and wake me up when it's time to leave.'* After dozing off for what seemed to be a split second, it was a challenge to muster the courage to plunge into the icy mountain air even if it was for a beautiful sunrise. Thankfully my sleepy self did not win and I thought to myself *'I didn't come this far just to sleep on top of Mt. Sinai! Come on, Belinda, get up and go out to see the sunrise! You know you'll regret it if you don't. Besides, isn't that why you dragged that silly camera around with you in the first place?'* True. Very true. So out I went and nestled myself in a narrow cleft in the huge, enormously huge mountain. It overlooked the other mountains and the valley from which we had climbed up. It was incredible. I had before me a 360° view of quiet serenity at the waking of a new day. Everyone became unusually silent. The sun was slowly pushing its way up onto the horizon and the colours splashed across the sky foretold its arrival. We all stood in awe, every one of us, absorbing the beauty and splendour. The moment the tip of the sun crossed the horizon, beams of light flooded the valleys and mountaintops. Everywhere I looked there were massive, rugged mountains that stood almost proudly as we gazed at them.

Soon the sun had gracefully floated well above the horizon and was steadily on its ascent as we prepared for our descent. At this point I was physically feeling a little better. Some of my strength seemed to have returned, just enough to function minimally and be alert. But generally speaking, I was like a zombie, exhausted beyond words and everything was happening in a haze. I had been awake all night, fighting with what felt like the whole host of fallen angels. I was a mess, but I was happy.

ENLIGHTENMENT

6:00-8:00

I heard the call 'Abdu!' and languidly stood to leave the crevice in the rock where I had been cocooned during the sunrise. I joined the rest of my group and our flock began its descent. The sun was up and I already felt as though I were in an oven. I walked down the same way I had gone up just a few hours earlier and what a relief it was to be going in the opposite direction. Again, camels stood on offer but I decided against them. I felt the descent and its weight on my knees. It strained the same muscles though in a different way, but I carried on. Now in broad daylight, I could see the path I had taken and I was in disbelief. I could not believe that I had come all that way, and in such a wretched state! Dumbfounded I stared down the side of the path, down the sharp edge of the mountain where the cliffs abruptly dropped. I could not even see the base. Had it been daylight during the ascent I have serious doubts about whether I would have carried on with such confidence and willpower. The mere sight of the soaring mountains all around and the steep, strenuous path that wound up and into an apparent infinity literally made me weak at the knees. Under the watchful eye of our Bedouin guide, I walked down at quite a steady and quick pace without stopping. There was nothing to absorb the intense heat of the scorching sun except our bodies; everything else was rock, rock, and more rocks. I arrived at the foot of the mountain in about two hours, as estimated.

8:00-9:00

St Catherine's Monastery was to open in an hour as it was also part of the tour. I looked around... Most people were sitting in the shade. Yearning to soak in as much sun before returning to dreary England, I was sitting in the sun, underestimating its strength. I was in what seemed to be a state between consciousness and sleep, something akin to being on autopilot, just waiting to go back to the hotel. I lay down on a stone wall and in my mind I flipped through the previous eight hours or so and wondered to what they had amounted. The trip seemed to be a haze of sweat, excessive exertion, thirst, fatigue, and psychological torment – one big battle to reach the top. Sure, it was worth it, no doubt about it. Yes, the sunrise was stunning and definitely worth seeing. And yes, overall it was an unforgettable experience. But from the back of my mind floated the thought about my spiritual quest, my personal pilgrimage to experience God. Where had He been in all that I had been doing? Where had He been during my eight hours of tremendous toil? Where was my spiritual enlightenment in what now seemed to be a disappointment rather than a triumph? Unexpectedly, what was supposed to be the climax seemed like the exact opposite. I could hear my hopes deflate as though from a wilted balloon.

Slowly, as though from a mist, thoughts began to emerge, though with a clarity far too unusual for my state of mind at that moment. I did my best to stay focused on them as they became clearer by the second. It was in that short interval of time that the revelation came, that the initial enlightenment of this experience unravelled and my spiritual expedition began to make sense. The pieces of the puzzle began to come together.

I messily scribbled oncoming thoughts onto a piece of paper I happened to have with me so that I would not forget them. What I first jotted down was this:

Limited visibility is to my advantage, even though I am not aware of it at the time.

Much like a child asking 'Are we there yet?', I had kept asking my guide, 'How much further? How much longer until we reach the summit?' and he told me to stop asking and keep going. This was not a pleasant thing to hear at the time and it was after those words that I knew there was still much further to go. It was such a strain for my eyes. I could not see much on the path and all that was illuminated by my flashlight was a circle of light right in front of me, a circle the size of your average pizza. I could not see far at all but I saw just enough to keep me going. As I climbed I kept wishing it were daylight so I could see the whole path, the whole mountain, and see where I was going. I wished I knew what I was dealing with and wanted to make it easier on myself. It was only as I began walking down that it dawned on me that my limited vision from earlier on had been a gift, a blessing in disguise. Had it all been revealed, I would have been terribly disheartened, to say the least. Had I seen where I was headed I would probably never have set foot on the mountain to begin with.

Often in my life I have complained about my circumstances. If only I knew more, if only God would tell me more, if only I knew what she was thinking, what he was planning, what would happen tomorrow, next year, in ten years, if only, if only, if only. If only I realised how *little* I understand what is truly good for me. What I most often complain about is most often precisely what is keeping me together. Advantage masquerades as disadvantage. Too often I get all hot and bothered at how things are, whining and getting angry at God who is not complying with my every demand when and how I see fit. God knows what He is doing. *God knows what He is doing.* It is not a mistake, a test-run or a fluke. If I invite Him to be my Guide, He accepts the invitation and all I need to do is follow His lead. I can have my questions and concerns, but follow anyway. In most cases I find the answers come faster than they would have otherwise. In hindsight I find I am always unbelievably grateful for it later, as I was in this case. Now when I am tempted to complain about poor visibility, wishing I knew more or could see further, I remember Mt. Sinai and do my best to focus on what I *do* see and keep walking.

Lying there in the sun I knew God was *re-interpreting* the night's events for me in a completely unexpected way. What had seemed a dreadful, all-around nightmare, was suddenly taking shape as what it truly was – God's way of answering my request. This toilsome climb was actually His way of honouring my search for Him, except in a way I had never expected. More often than not I need this re-interpretation but do not necessarily ask for it. I want God's input, I want Him around, but more as a passive observer, as a 'nice guy' who leads when I need Him to but whom I ignore as soon as He gets in my way. I examine my life events and situations, replaying them in my mind a million times over and always see them in the same way, assigning them the same values and meanings. But what if that is not the whole picture? What if there is another interpretation of a specific event, another way of looking at my entire life that I am not able to see right now? God's re-interpretation, the way things *really* are, can and has changed the lives of many, mine included. Even when things are tough, knowing what is *really* going on helps more than I thought it would. As I reflected further, it dawned on me that

When I am at my weakest, help comes in unexpected packaging.

I was at my weakest up there on those steps, where so many others were giving up and letting go. At one point I literally used both my hands and feet to climb upwards. More often than not I faltered, I crawled more than I walked. Our guide Magda had significantly helped me. I know that is his job but regardless, he was my help when I needed it. However what was certainly more unexpected was the forever-anonymous Bedouin who appeared when I was at my lowest. When I was sprawled out on those steps, aching all over and on the verge of tears, he approached me. At first I rejected his help, finding plenty of rational reasons to cement my choice. After all, if nothing else, when I was a child my mother had taught me to be careful when speaking to strangers and this was a strange man. I was alone (in a manner of speaking), in the dark; this could have spelt disaster in another scenario. Instead he offered me his sincere help and was true to his word. He took my arm and together we walked, at my pace, as far as I could go. It is safe to say that I could not have completed the climb without him.

The help I need often comes in unexpected packaging. Often it is through people and situations I do not imagine would be helpful that God chooses to reach out to me. Sometimes all it takes is a sentence spoken by someone unexpected and things fall into place for me; I recognise His voice and the message for what it is. History has shown that God has an infinite number of ways in which to manifest, so I have found it worthwhile to keep my eyes and ears open, so to speak. If I rigidly stick to my notions of how God talks to me, how He is 'supposed' to communicate with me, then I am limiting Him and I am also quite likely to completely miss the help He is sending!

When I reach my goal, I realise it is most definitely worth the effort.

Everything about being on the top of Mt. Sinai that early morning was simply incredible. The air crisp and cool, the atmosphere reverent in its silence. Mountaintops stretched before me as far as the eye could see. Captivating. From what seemed like an infinite distance, the wild and rugged mountains gave way to the grand and elegant sun. I was witnessing the birth of a new day in a spectacular way; it was a moment of humility, wonder and gratitude. It was worth it. As the sun was rising, the intensity of the memories from just a few hours before were fading. What had seemed futile and unbearable now seemed incomparable to the beauty I was experiencing. What had been toilsome labour was something for which I was now deeply thankful. As difficult as my journey had been, it was a gift in unexpected packaging, an effort greatly rewarded – truly beyond my imagination.

As I was scribbling these pearls of wisdom lying on that hot, stone wall, I thought back to the dynamic of climbing and resting, and a crucial idea emerged.

Find a balance – rest just enough to gather your strength, but not for too long; for each time I rest it becomes more difficult to continue.

I mentioned that I had broken out in a sweat quite early on and that it had persisted during the entire climb. The beads of sweat on my face that I regularly wiped with my sleeve were evidence of the effort I was exerting; they were proof of my difficulties. I longed for rest and so I did rest, here and there, for short periods of time, just enough to catch my breath and continue the gruesome trek. When I paused to rest, sweaty and fatigued, the chilly wind blew and I would begin to shake. There was just no place to be comfortable! If the aches and pains of climbing did not beset me, the shivers of resting tormented me instead. I noticed that every time I rested it was harder to get going again. At these times it seemed as though my body began to yell and scream at me, demanding to be heard and taken into consideration. I was tired, hungry, thirsty and wanted to properly rest, not just for a minute or two. I dared not stay idle for too long. I had to force myself to continue climbing while a part of me still longed to stay behind. It was willpower and nothing else that forced me to go on with the climb.

Finding a balance in life is difficult. Some of us are so busy we are running around with no time to rest, always on the move, making, chasing, scheming, planning, organising, ticking boxes on endless lists, climbing whatever our mountain may be at the moment. Rest, true rest, is a commodity we do not seem to have time for. It is for the weak, for sissies, for those who are not visionaries and go-getters like we are. On the other hand, others among us are so busy resting that we have not moved an inch in the last ten, twenty, or even fifty years. Monotony, self-pity, and a lack of motivation have beset us. We have taken ourselves out of the climb. We are sitting on our rock so occupied by resting that our mountain remains unconquered, our horizons 'un-widened', our experience 'un-riched'. We have become like a swamp, a stinking body of water that has no flow, no direction, headed nowhere. Which one are you? Why? (I was both, I was busy being stuck). How are we to find a balance? The answer to that alone could easily take up more space than this book allows, but I find the crux of it is this: the better my connection is with my Guide, the better my chance is of finding and *living* this balance. Not just talking about it, wishing for it, but truly *living* it.

There will always be camels; there will always be an easier option but it is not necessarily the best one.

Just when I thought the camels and their Bedouins had disappeared and left me alone, there they were again, whispering and taunting me, a clever decoy from my firm resolve. Like an arrow shot from a bow, their helpful offer was aimed at my weakest point and I was vulnerable. Time and again I had to say no, politely declining the offer and each time reassuring myself I was making the right decision, reassuring myself I would make it to the top and that it would be worth climbing every inch of it.

Make no mistake, this is no trivial matter. What I was wrestling with that night, all night long, it seems, happens to all of us perhaps more often than we realise. Now as I look back on my Sinai adventure countless sunrises later, I know this to be truer than ever before. I do not know what you are battling at the moment – the pivotal point over which you spend sleepless nights, hours of worry and anxiety – but perhaps the reality of it is the same. Perhaps you too, like me, are being called either to *follow,* or *to give up*. It is usually one or the other and it manifests in seemingly trivial ways, like mine did on this climb. After all this was 'just a climb' and the world would not stop spinning if I did not reach the top. On the outside yes, but on the inside, things would have been starkly different had I chosen the alternative.

Sometimes the decisions I face seem mundane and trivial and at face value they do not seem to have grave consequences. But I have learnt that before I make my move, before I cut cords and take a leap, I make sure I have taken the iPod out of my ears and turned off all the buzz and hubbub that surrounds me. I try to bring myself to a place of peace and quiet and then listen. What else is there? Is there something I might be missing? Is there a crucial element in my story I have not considered until now? I might have been careful, and this will only be a precaution. But on the chance that I have not, on the chance that something is obscured from view, something that could change things, it is worth looking into. There is often more at stake than meets the eye.

How many camels are on your path right now? What are they? I imagine they are perfectly suited to your needs, masquerading as help and not hindrance, playing to your vulnerabilities like they do to mine. There will always be camels, every day of my life and there will be varying alternatives and choices I will have to make. The question is, 'Which is the better option, and how am I to know the difference?'

In my story, my *method* of climbing was *connected* to my *goal* – to hear from God, to fully engage in the process and hopefully experience God's guidance and will for my life. Bearing that in mind, to have yielded to the camels would have been to diminish the process, to weaken my own resolve and to expect something from God with almost no effort on my part. It seemed presumptuous and unnecessary, though naturally more comfortable. Since my goal was to experience God in a deeper sense, I trusted He would sustain me as I climbed, I trusted Him to help me reach the top. To have taken a camel would have been to doubt God's ability to do just that and I know it would have changed the entire experience.

Yes, God can work wonderful things from my errors and He has and He does, but I have found that I often *underestimate the necessity of the process*. I do not always easily or immediately understand how beneficial or valuable it is for me. It is the process, above all else, that is of paramount importance. Henry Wadsworth Longfellow said, 'Perseverance is a great element of success. If you only knock long enough and loud enough at the gate, you are sure to wake up somebody.'

I climbed that mountain with both of my feet (and sometimes my hands) and that experience became embedded in me. It was real, smelling of sweat, exhaustion and sheer willpower. I would not have had such a hard time had I taken a camel but I would not have known the reality of the struggle either. I would not have appreciated the mountain for what it represented. I would have missed so much without even knowing it. I am not always going to faultlessly let Him lead; I know this struggle from my own life. But there is a way in which I can become aware of what is being offered and ask myself, 'Will this lead me closer to God or farther away?' The difference might be frighteningly subtle.

The crowd was steadily growing restless, eager to enter the monastery and find shelter from the blazing sun. I had one last thing to note down.

When light reveals what was previously in darkness, I realise how far I have come and know that I did not arrive there alone.

Would you agree that progress is very often intangible? A child's growth is noticeable in many ways. They go to school, study, get good marks and move up to the next grade. As they grow physically they are taller and the progress is easily monitored with a pencil, tape measure and a wall. But as an adult it seems that progress becomes much more of an abstract phenomenon. It seems society teaches us to measure progress by external markers. Consequently as an individual I am often led to believe that because I was not given that promotion I wanted and because I now cannot afford that holiday or house or whatever, I have not progressed very far; I am stuck in the same spot. It could very well be, but dare I say that I can get that promotion, fancy holiday and house and still be stuck. *When exactly did you and I stop thinking of **progress** as a **process** and instead focus on the end product as its sole measure?* In other words, why is a process not deemed as good an indicator of progress as is the end product?

Climbing that mountain for hours on end, in the dark, working towards something I knew only abstractly, it was difficult to monitor my progress; in fact it was almost impossible. Behind me: darkness, ahead of me: darkness. Progress? In the pitch black of that night it seemed that if there was any progress at all it was from bad to worse!

All that changed when the sun came up and daylight revealed what had been enveloped in darkness. Obscure became evident, elusive became tangible – my progress was real. I looked below, staring down at the path I had taken up the mountain; I had climbed all that way! Wow! I was stunned. That was a lot! I had come very far, very high and I could not have even imagined just how far and how high. Even as I stared down, astounded, I was aware I had not made it alone. I had come a long way and it was with the help of others, each playing a role in my climb. Most of all, it was God who had sustained me and helped me through the mental battles, who had enabled me to persevere and stick unwaveringly to my course. He had been there all along as I struggled with so many things simultaneously. He had been there and now it was even more obvious that He had. I had asked for His unmistakable presence and He had graciously offered it. Sometimes progress is only perceptible when light is shed on what has passed and the bigger picture emerges, when each component falls into place and things can be seen for what they really are.

09:00

The monastery had now opened and the hot and flustered masses flocked to the entrance. I had jotted down all that had come to me. It centred on six key thoughts that summarised my entire Sinai experience. I knew even then that it had been God's answer to my request, His response to my search. I had not yet fully delved into these thoughts to grasp their complete meaning but, exhausted as I was, I happily put away my paper and pencil and headed for the shade of the monastery. I had received what I had come for and more. I was deeply content, I was at peace and I knew God was near.

*   *   *

CONCLUSIONS

Since that night many years ago, I often look back and ponder the way God chose to speak to me that night. Every time I come back to it, this experience deepens, its narrative grows richer and its message becomes more meaningful.

That said, I remember a time when the notion of hearing from God was not so simple and definitely not so clear. There are people (and I was one of them many years ago) who assume that in principle God does speak and communicates somehow, but when it comes to them personally, in the 21st century, that is where things begin to get hazy. For many, as it once was for me, that subject is a source of quiet anxiety, confusion and frustration. It is something akin to sitting next to a radio, trying to find the desired frequency, hoping that somehow we will stumble upon the right one and God will be speaking through it. But none of that process seems clear or certain, and so many remain unsure about how this communication with God actually works (or is supposed to work, if at all). Is our radio good enough? Is the frequency there but do we keep missing it? And if perchance we find it, how can we be sure to find it again? What I am about to say will expand and build on the underlying assumptions I held that night as I climbed, and will hopefully begin to further untangle some of the messy threads of this notion of God speaking to us. In order to better understand it we will first need to delve into the human brain. Follow me there if you will.

Our brain consists of two halves that are linked together by a thick bundle of nerves known as the *corpus callosum,* often compared to a motorway with multiple lanes. In the last few decades much research has gone into the specificities of each hemisphere – which one does what and how (though the question of cerebral lateralisation, as it is known, has been of interest for much longer). In the early years scientists were discovering that certain functionalities seemed to be linked with particular parts of the brain (the left and/or the right) and so the idea of a 'split mind' began to grow. As the research advanced so did the idea of the divided consciousness. This idea grew to the extent that instead of the brain and mind being considered one complex structure, it was now viewed and discussed as two almost entirely disconnected halves, each with separate and opposite personalities, completely alienated one from the other. The matter of cerebral dominance also spilled over into the notion of handedness and numerous studies followed on how the hemispheres impacted dexterity, asking questions such as how similar or different left-handed individuals were from right-handed individuals.[1]

As a result the research of the brain's hemispheres comes with somewhat of a bittersweet taste because often the 'left vs. right' has reached mythic proportions and ironically perpetuated further dichotomies instead of bringing it all together into the larger story of the whole brain. The good news is that this lop-sidedness was recognised by the research community and over the years attempts have been made to emphasise that the human mind "[…] is a complex phenomenon built on the physical scaffolding of the brain […]".[2] [3]

In that same vein we are reminded by leading cognitive neuroscientist Professor Michael S. Gazzaniga that

"[…] even though each cerebral hemisphere has its own set of capacities, with the left hemisphere specialized for language and speech and major problem-solving capacities and the right hemisphere specialized for tasks such as facial recognition and attentional monitoring, we all have the subjective experience of feeling totally integrated."[4]

---

[1] In fact Prof. Chris McManus wrote a fascinating book on lateralisation as it relates to handedness and in it he addresses many interesting questions such as: Why are most people right-handed? Why don't identical twins always have the same dominant hand? Why are some scripts written left to right and others right to left? Prof. McManus even starts chapter 9 with a Biblical reference to Ehud, son of Gera the Benjamite, who was left-handed! *Right Hand, Left Brain: The Origins of Asymmetry in Brains, Bodies, Atoms and Cultures*, (London: Weinfeld & Nicolson, 2002).

[2] D. S. Bassett and M. S. Gazzaniga, "Understanding complexity in the human brain", *Trends in Cognitive Sciences* 15(5)(2011), 200-209.

[3] A well-known example that attempted to restore some balance was *The Integrated Mind* written in 1978 by Prof. Michael S. Gazzaniga and Prof. Joseph E. LeDoux (New York, NY: Plenum Press). For those of you who might like to pursue this further, Prof. Gazzaniga has quite recently published a behind-the-scenes book of his life and research entitled *Tales from both sides of the brain: a life in neuroscience* (New York, NY: Ecco/HarperCollins, 2015).

[4] Michael S. Gazzaniga, "Cerebral specialization and interhemispheric communication: Does the corpus callosum enable the human condition?", *Brain* 123(7)(2000), 1293-1326.

In other words, specificities aside, our brain functions seamlessly as a whole and there is still much that remains to be discovered. What we do know, however, is that contrary to the prevalent opinion of the past few hundred years (if not more), neither half is 'better' or 'more important' than the other. As Dr Oliver Sacks puts it, "[...] they [the hemispheres] are merely suited for different dimensions and stages of processing. Both are complementary, interacting [...]."[5]

For better or worse, "The dichotomy between so-called left-brain and right-brain styles of thinking is now thoroughly engrained in our folklore."[6] The question is: what will we do with it? I agree with psychologist Michael Corballis when he says that despite efforts to maintain what is hopefully a balanced and objective view it is nevertheless difficult to claim any special immunity to it. Therefore in this book I will not claim immunity nor will I add to existing dichotomies. However what I will do is use the idea of the hemispheres as a means of highlighting different ways of experiencing the world. This will serve as a diving board off which to jump into a world that is the *totality* of our experience.

Taking all that into consideration, before continuing let me insert a disclaimer here. The view presented in this book is not intended as part of any potential discussions of left 'brain' versus right 'brain' nor in the exalting of one over the other. My following use of the terms 'right hemisphere' (RH hereon) and 'left hemisphere' (LH hereon) is admittedly simplistic in the strictly physiological sense, but my purpose here is not to provide a comprehensive physiological explanation (although there are pointers for that). Rather, my aim is that of an analogous kind, intended to portray the different human cognitive processes that shape the ways in which we function and engage the inner and outer world.

Brain scientist Dr Jill Bolte Taylor suffered a stroke when a blood vessel ruptured in her left hemisphere leaving her with only her right hemisphere intact. It took her eight years to completely recover and regain functionality of her entire brain, but it gave her the opportunity to uniquely observe her own mind and get to know the two hemispheres more intimately. Since

---

[5] Oliver Sacks, *Seeing Voices*, (Berkley: University of California Press; London: Picador, 1989), 106.
[6] Michael C. Corballis, *Human Laterality*, (New York, NY: Academic Press, 1983), 7.

she so eloquently describes them both, I will use her words to convey the 'personalities' of each hemisphere to you before we continue.[7]

The Right Hemisphere

It is free to think outside the box, creatively explores the possibilities that each new moment brings. Spontaneous and carefree, its imaginative and artistic juices can flow without inhibition or judgment. It thinks in pictures and gives a context to everything else, aware of 'the big picture'. It is empathetic and loves humanity; it can walk in the shoes of another and cares about other people's feelings. It knows that somehow, we are all connected. It is adventurous, socially adept, and very good at understanding nonverbal communication and decoding emotion. It is highly creative, always willing to try something new and can appreciate chaos. It is intuitive, tuned in to the subtle messages our cells communicate via gut feelings. It is kinaesthetic, biologically designed to readily tune into our physiology. It loves the body's ability to move freely in the world and it learns through touch and experience. It is all about the present moment.

The Left Hemisphere

It prides itself in being very good at organising things, judging, critically analysing them. It is busy theorising, rationalising and memorising. For our perfectionist left mind, everything has its place and everything belongs in its place. It is gifted at identifying patterns and processing information

---

[7] Descriptions based on chapters three and sixteen of Jill Bolte Taylor, *My Stroke of Insight*, (London: Hodder & Stoughton, Ltd., 2006), 37-47, 137-146. For more on what is also known as the dual process theory of human intelligence, see S. Epstein, R. Pacini, V. Denes-Raj, and H. Heier, "Individual differences in intuitive-experiential and analytical-rational thinking styles", *Journal of Personality and Social Psychology*, 71 (1996), 290-405. The 'intelligence' in this theory stems from the notion that the individual can successfully and easily switch between the two modes of thinking. S. B. Kaufmann, "Intelligence and the cognitive unconscious" in *The Cambridge handbook of intelligence*, eds. R. J. Steinberg and S. B. Kaufmann, (New York: Cambridge University Press, 2011), 442. I do not necessarily share all Dr Bolte Taylor's spiritual interpretations and implications of her experience, but I do find her experience valuable which is why I have included it in the book.

remarkably fast. It is designed to weave stories and make sense of the world outside of us based on minimal information. It is interested in details, and details of details and it linearly and methodically deals with information. Its language centres use words to describe, define, categorise and communicate about everything. It excels in academics and honours our uniqueness, striving for independence. It thinks in terms of the past, present and the future.

As you read the above descriptions I am sure it brought a smile or two across your face because in one way or another, you could identify those attributes in yourself. Whether we tend to be more creative or more organised, curious about 'the big picture' or the details of it, is partly due to our personality, our current life situation, the kind of environment in which we were raised, and which attributes were valued more than others.

Whether we gravitate towards one or the other, as both Dr Bolte Taylor and other researchers of the brain's hemispheres say, "[…] when normally connected, the two hemispheres complement and enhance one another's abilities."[8] It is not a competition; it is about complementarity and cooperation. As you are reading this, your left hemisphere is analysing the words on the page, deciphering the structure of the words while your right hemisphere is tuned in to my tone of voice, the underlying emotion behind the words on the page. In order for you to fully grasp the meaning of what you are reading, you need both hemispheres to do what they do best, and that is true not only of reading but of life in general.

Let me emphasise that we need our *whole* brain in order to function optimally and one hemisphere can never take the place of the other. I am not advocating the superiority of the right over the left hemisphere in any way, after all they are *one* brain. As I said before, I am advocating the *totality* of our daily experience.

«There should not be any sense of the concrete and the abstract as mutually exclusive, of the one being abandoned as one progresses to the other. On the contrary, it is precisely the richness of the concrete that gives power to the abstract.»[9]

---

[8] "By recognizing who is who inside our cranium, we can take a more *balanced-brain* approach to how we lead our lives." Bolte Taylor, *My Stroke of Insight*, 133.
[9] Sacks, *Seeing Voices*, 124.

The reason why my emphasis may perhaps seem to be more on the RH is simply because ever since brain lateralisation became of interest (back in the 19th century), for a long time the RH was considered 'merely a weaker version of the left' or ignored all together.[10] This heavy emphasis on the LH has been to our detriment, as neuroscientist Rodolfo Llinás informs us that:

«The neural processes underlying that which we call creativity have nothing to do with rationality. That is to say, if we look at how the brain generates creativity, we will see that it is not a rational process at all; creativity is not born out of reasoning.»[11]

The point I am about to make is very important. This book is ultimately not about the hemispheres, neither their anatomy nor their complex history. But as brain scientists Andrew Newberg, Eugene D'Acquili and Vince Rause point out in their book and what my climb up Mt. Sinai showed me is:

«There's no other way for God to get into your head except through the brain's neural pathways.»[12]

In other words, limiting God to a certain set of neural pathways

---

[10] Arthur Benton, "Perception of Direction in the Right and Left Visual Fields," *Neuropsychologia*, Vol. 10 (1972), 447-452. French neuroanatomist and anthropologist Paul Broca (1824-1880), was at the time dealing with cases of people who had experienced damage to their frontal lobe and as a result lost the ability to speak. This pointed to a connection between speech loss and damage to the *left* side of the brain. Broca had difficulty accepting the idea that there could be two (apparently) identical structures that functioned differently so eventually this discovery led to the opinion that the left side of the brain is the "intelligent" and "educated" side. In the 1870s cases revealed the role of the right hemisphere in emotion (including hysterical manifestations which were common at the time) and soon the right hemisphere was seen as the "emotional" side of the brain that also harboured "basic irrationalist tendencies that could lead to madness". Richard J. Davidson and Kenneth Hugdahl, eds. *Brain Asymmetry*, (Cambridge, MA: MIT, 1996), 12-13.
[11] Rodolfo R. Llinás, *I of the Vortex: From Neurons to Self*, (Cambridge, MA: MIT Press, 2002), 170.
[12] Andrew Newberg, M.D., Eugene D'Acquili, M.D., Ph.D., and Vince Rause, *Why God Won't Go Away: Brain Science & the Biology of Belief*, (New York, NY: Ballatine Books, 2002), 37.

(through our habitual ways of thinking and being) is precisely that: limiting. The aim of this book–and certainly this part of the book–is to broaden our spectrum of experience (of ourselves and of God), and to discover new pathways instead of merely cementing existing ones.

Newberg, D'Acquili and Rause neatly highlight that

«Both hemispheres of the brain are capable of some kind of awareness, but their methods of experiencing and expressing it are very different.»[13]

and it is this point of view that is taken as the basis for this book; one complex mind that does things in a myriad of diverse ways.

To me our 21st century world seems to be very much about clean lines, glass, metal, sharp edges, cold and sleek. Those attributes are not to be discarded but it seems to me that we could do with more soul, spirit, joy, depth, curves and warmth. With each passing day it seems more crucial that we reclaim our intuition, our body, our senses, and the totality of experience that stems from living life with our whole brain, our whole being. In doing so it will restore balance and reintroduce us to a way of being that while native to us, has long been neglected. That is what this part of the book endeavours to help you do – slowly bring ways of experiencing the world (usually associated with the RH) out of hiding and into the light of day where they will amaze and enrapture you. As you engage with your whole brain, you are likely to find it will awaken things within you that have been dormant for much too long a time.

The reason I find this so important is because it seems to me that we are living as though we suffered from agnosia,[14] except in our case it is not visual or auditory, it is *hemispherical*. What do I mean? I mean that for the most part of every day, we trudge along living our lives though using

---

[13] Newberg, D'Acquili, and Rause, *Why God Won't Go Away,* 23.

[14] *Agnosia* (literally meaning 'not knowing') is a defect in recognition. Generally, an agnosic can sense objects and forms but cannot consciously recognize and interpret their meaning. A person with agnosia will see members of their family or even parts of their own body but will not be able to recognize them as such. Agnosia is the result of a neurological pathology and can be manifested in any cognitive/perceptual system (e.g. visual, tactile, auditory…). For an interesting read concerning a type of agnosia, read about Dr P. in Oliver Sacks, *The Man Who Mistook His Wife for a Hat*, (London: Picador, 2011). There is a 2015 edition available.

both hemispheres, emphasising predominantly the qualities associated with our left hemisphere whilst those typically associated with our right one are severely neglected. In some individuals it is worse than in others. *'Hemispherical agnosia'*, as I have termed it, is the neglect of one aspect of ourselves, i.e. the neglect of a vast palette of human experience, and a rather important one, too. Sadly, instead of taking full advantage of the whole brain we rely heavily on just a part of it and thereby sell ourselves short of many insights, joys, and discoveries.[15]

As children we are all creative, keen on discovering and exploring ourselves and our surroundings, and we find joy in the smallest of things. Joy seems accessible and this way with the world is natural for us. We scribble and draw and colour in, we play music, sing, dance, we love telling and hearing stories, we make cakes of mud, swords of sticks, palaces of branches and we are happy. That is because we *are*, and because it *is* our second nature. Both our hemispheres are talking to each other regularly, and our view of the world is fuller, more rounded and complete. But then one day we go to school where we are taught that maths and science are more important (at least implicitly), more valuable than imagination, art and creativity, and slowly it begins. The RH begins to slide offstage into darkness as the LH comes on centre stage as the star. The one is fed and grows while the other slowly starves. Before we know it we are adults and for some reason we have a hard time drawing, singing or dancing as we once did, it just does not flow and we feel silly, even embarrassed. When our boss asks for a more creative solution to a problem we are perplexed and wonder what it even means to be creative anymore. What was once effortless is now strenuous (if we are even brave enough to attempt it). Perhaps we have even forgotten how much we loved and enjoyed all those 'silly' things when we were children. Why am I mentioning all of this? Bear with me for a second and follow me closely.

If God had done what I had expected Him to – if I had had a more

---

[15] Of course the opposite can be true, in which one neglects the LH and emphasises the RH to the detriment of the whole. There is perhaps a case to be made about this, but I have chosen to describe an agnosia that involves the suppression or exclusion of the RH, based on the evidence that the LH has become more prominent for reasons that should partly be clear by now, but will also become more evident as the book unfolds. I find the hemispherical lop-sidedness to be particularly in favour of the LH in Western religious and Biblical discourse.

comfortable climb and heard Him speak to me in words, in thoughts and ideas – I would have processed it with my linear, analytical left hemisphere, as information received. This is not necessarily a bad thing because after all, we need both halves of our brain and the specific advantages they both bring in order to function optimally. Instead what happened was the complete opposite: God chose to speak to me through my right hemisphere and I did not recognise it for what it was.[16] You see, during my climb I was there, fully present in the situation, physically, emotionally and mentally. I felt every ache and pain, every bead of sweat, every gasping breath. I was completely engaged. This is what was happening as I was climbing: I was encoding that night as an *experience*, of sounds, smells, thoughts, feelings and images. It was being implicitly stored in my brain as *nonverbal* information. That is why, as I climbed, expecting to hear from God in a more structured, *verbal* way, I was a little discouraged when it did not happen and wondered how it was all going to turn out. I had no time for philosophical musings on the nature of revelation, God or anything else for that matter; it was all very vivid, concrete and unforgettable.

It was only in the morning on that stone wall that God began to activate my left hemisphere and helped me become more aware of my nocturnal experience more explicitly. Nonverbal and verbal were joining forces; the two hemispheres were sharing in active communication. The nonverbal was being articulated in verbal form and what emerged were those six thoughts that summarised the nonverbal experience. It was because of this that I gained a fuller, rounder, more complete understanding of what had transpired. I marvelled. Wow! What a surprise! I was taken aback. God knew what He was doing all along. It took me a while to catch on but, thanks to Him, I eventually did. I was in search of a deeper connection, a revelation and an experience that would draw me closer to Him. I wanted it to be real and to be personal – and it was all that and more.[17]

---

[16] "The right hemisphere's role [...] is critical for dealing with novel situations, for which there does not yet exist any established descriptive system or code [...]" Sacks, *Seeing Voices*, 105.

[17] This movement from right to left hemisphere seems to occur more frequently than we would imagine. In the person who has suffered a great trauma (and PTSD results), the trauma gets 'stuck' in the nonverbal RH, frozen in time, making it very difficult for the person to verbally access it. Through the use of RH-geared techniques the traumatic material can be tapped into and begun to be shared and dealt with

You see, if God had spoken to me as I had expected (in words and thoughts typical of the LH) and had brought those six key thoughts into my mind as I climbed, I would have registered them, perhaps thought about them for a moment or two, perhaps longer, and that would have been that. They would have gone only skin deep. But on the other hand, if He had spoken to me only through the aches and pains and sweat and of it (RH), I would have left Mt. Sinai wondering where God had been; I would not have been able to discern His hand in it at all. In other words, if God had spoken in *only* one way, typically associated with only one hemisphere, left or right, *it would not have been enough*. It would have been half a message, if that. So He masterfully engaged my whole brain, first the RH then the LH. In doing so He engaged my *whole self*. First I experienced the mountain and then He gave me His commentary; *He transformed my experience into words and thoughts that made sense of it all*. Genius.

As I mentioned earlier, in the few years since my climb I have come to value this experience even more than I did back then. It has become a kind of blueprint which I refer back to, to remind me of how God is, how He surprises me and always in a good way, how things are often not what they seem and how I need Him to do things His way because He has proven time and again that *He knows what He is doing*. In just one night so much had changed. My longing had been fulfilled and I had truly experienced God. I am not saying I magically became a person who was no longer broken or without my fair share of problems to plough through, not at all, but I had experienced something priceless on that mountain, something I carry with me to this day. I got to know God a little better; I walked with Him and He walked with me. He gave me insight into the

---

(Savneet Talwar, "Accessing Traumatic Memory Through Art Making: An Art Therapy Trauma Protocol (ATTP)", *The Arts in Psychotherapy*, Vol. 34 (2007), 22-35. As mentioned above, much (though not all) of our linguistic deciphering happens in the left hemisphere that controls all processes that are organised such as grammars and codes. Interestingly, Dr Sacks points out that even though a novel linguistic task (which we would expect to be processed by the left hemisphere), will initially be processed mostly by the right hemisphere. Later on, as that task becomes routinised, it will move over and become a function of the left hemisphere. For example, "[...] while musical perception is mainly a right hemisphere function predominantly in 'naïve' listeners, it becomes a left hemisphere function in professional musicians and 'expert' listeners (who grasp its 'grammar' and rules, and for whom it has become an intricate formal structure)." Sacks, *Seeing Voices*, 105-106.

dynamic of how we relate to each other. I have since enjoyed many more adventures with God and we have grown much closer, He and I. I have learnt to discern when He speaks much more clearly, and He has proven to be more real and more personal than I had ever dreamt possible. And though I am still learning and have gotten things wrong many times since then, the memory of that night has strengthened me and speaks to me in countless ways, to this very day.

What about you, what is your mountain?
Do you long for a deeper, more meaningful connection with God?
Do you want a God who is real and personal?
Do you want to hear Him speak to *you*?

He is available and within reach; the experience you long for is not a dream, unattainable or make-believe and it is not for an elect few. He is right here, waiting, and He *will* surprise you. I invite you to climb your mountain, whatever it may be, to invest yourself fully, to go all the way, no turning back. I challenge you to persevere in your quest for a full life and a deeper connection with Him. Dare to be curious about what could happen if you stepped out into the unknown with Him. I encourage you to follow His lead, even if it be by the more painful route (and it usually is) and trust Him with the process. It might just be the best choice you will ever make...

*   *   *

YOUR CREATIVE JOURNEY

After everything you have read so far, you might be wondering how exactly one goes about activating the 'right hemisphere' and indeed the whole brain and self to a greater degree. How does one go from wishing for it to actually making it happen? How can we live fuller lives?

As I mentioned in the introduction, this next part of the book will show you just that – how to practically and purposefully engage your whole brain and leave you with tangible tools you can apply to any area of your life.

This part of the book has also come about as a result of my own personal journey and I have decided to share a part of it with you. You may or may not consider yourself as spiritual or religious, you may feel ambiguous in regard to God, He may seem distant and inaccessible, or it just may be that you are looking for some direction in life and are not sure how to go about it… Whatever your situation, I trust you will find something valuable for your own journey in what follows.

What awaits you on the pages to follow are stepping stones of a creative path intended to lead you closer to God and a greater understanding of yourself.[18] Should you choose to go on this journey with me, you will focus on certain topics each day using creative ways to contemplate and express what is happening within.[19] By exploring the topics creatively you will be activating both, but predominantly your right hemisphere, and the subsequent analysis prompted by questions will activate more of your left hemisphere.[20] The movement will be from nonverbal to verbal,

---

[18] There are 33 days of this creative path and the reason for that number is purely because they have been based on my own journals and not particularly chosen for the number itself.

[19] You might not manage every day, or you might find that you will want to linger on one day or exercise for longer, which is fine. The idea is simply to do this continually, so even if you do not do them every day, try to maintain a certain rhythm to it in order to gain the maximum benefit.

[20] "Discovery learning leads to intuitive knowledge. It cannot ever be produced by merely verbal learning; it can only be acquired through experiential involvement of the subject in a practical or mental activity." Efraim Fischbein, *Intuition in science and mathematics*, (Dordrecht, The Netherlands: Reidel, 1987), 95.

experiential to analytical, concrete to abstract. The two will be called forth to communicate, one informing the other of its findings and help you *begin to experience life and God in a deeper and richer way*. Be faithful to the process because it is the *process* that will have its effect, not just one passage or one day in isolation. Commit to complete it and you might just be surprised at what discoveries you unearth and the positive changes you notice in and around you.

As I mentioned, each day you will be exploring a certain topic based on a Bible passage and you will notice that most of the passages are from the Old Testament/Hebrew Bible. I know that unfortunately many people familiar with the Bible, consciously or unconsciously, make a distinction between the Old and New Testaments, often understanding the God of the Old Testament to be harsh, severe, one who punishes and destroys, while the God of the New Testament is perceived as loving, kind, gentle and understanding. If you are one of those people, I invite you to set aside your reservations and go into this with an open mind. I trust that in the pages to come you will discover dimensions of God in the Old Testament you may have previously overlooked, and will come to recognise, perhaps more than before, the same character traits of the 'New Testament God' in the 'Old Testament God'.

You do not have to be artistically talented whatsoever in order to enjoy and take full advantage of this journey, so do carry on. What you will need, though, is the following:

o   colouring pencils
o   a notebook or journal you will use just for this purpose
o   a pen and/or pencil

Two things need to be said before we begin. The first one is that I have noticed time and again that most of us adults have a hard time letting go when it comes to artistic undertakings and tend to get too analytical, think too much before we begin drawing, afraid what others would say if they saw our work… This is part of the plague of the heavy emphasis on the LH and is exactly what these exercises are going to attempt to help you balance out. So bear in mind: when it comes to the practical exercises *resist the urge to think* and just go with the flow, draw what comes, let it come naturally and do not worry, your artwork is a personal, creative expression of yourself and is valuable as such. The less you analyse and think, the freer your RH will be and the more you will actually enjoy the process! Asterisks like this * will separate the practical exercises from the subsequent analysis, so when you reach the asterisks, be sure to do the exercises *before* moving on.[21]

The second one is that there is only one prerequisite to doing this and that is: you have to want to do it. If you *do* want to embark on this journey by all means please continue... The will of a human being is a potent thing. If you find you are not particularly inspired to engage it, if for whatever reason you are not fully interested in pursuing it right now, leave it. Come back to it another time. Without you *wanting* to do this, this process will cause aggravation and hindrance instead of progress.[22]

Think of today as a *preparation day* for what you are about to begin. A clear, uncluttered mind and heart do not magically happen, even if God is involved. We are what we watch, eat, drink, think and feel. I can technically be vegan by eating crisps and guzzling fizzy drinks all day, but I would only be kidding myself and not really doing myself any favours.

Just as you do before travelling anywhere, you pack, organise yourself, sort out your belongings (even if it is the night before)... do the same here. Before embarking on this journey, do your best to rid your life of unnecessary clutter and take with you only what you really need.

Since we are affected by our physical environment, by what we ingest, how we sleep, what we are exposed to each day, below are some bonus points for those of you who are up for an extra challenge. We are not a sum of parts but rather a complex whole, so anything that is good for you will spill over into other areas of your life.

---

[21] When driving on a dirt road with deep grooves in the soil it is difficult to maneuver onto another path. So it is with the hemispheres; if you proceed to the analysis questions before completing the exercise it is highly likely you will inhibit your RH. You will fall into the neuronal grooves of the linear LH and 'de-activate' the completely different *modus operandi* of the RH.

[22] "No integration, no individuation, no healing, no spiritual development, no conversion, no renewal, no rebirth – nothing whatever in the area of psychic growth – is possible without receptivity. Receptivity – or in any case a will to the same, however diminutive, however tentative – makes sick persons well, gets derailed psyches back on track, makes the dull wise." Hanna Wolff, *Jesus the Therapist*, (RADIUS-Verlag, GmbH, Stuttgart, 1978), 86-87.

o   Eat wholesome, nutritious food (breakfast included) so that your brain will be in top form, getting the energy it needs so you will have clarity, concentration and be more inclined to experience the creative flow.

o   Be physically active, exercise, walk in the forest, by the sea, in the park, breathe in fresh air, stretch.[23]

o   Get enough good sleep if possible. Listen to your body when it is yawning and telling you it would be a good idea if you went to bed.[24]

o   Do a mini spring-cleaning session of your room or personal space (especially the one in which you will mostly be spending time during these exercises) – less physical clutter helps regulate mental clutter.

o   Give yourself some silent time during the day... you would be surprised what floats to the surface when it is not drowned out by noise (if you dare, turn off your TV, radio, iPod etc. and notice how this silent time will positively impact you).

These suggestions are not of paramount importance, but if you adhere to at least some of them you will undoubtedly feel the benefits along the way.

Whether you set aside time in the morning or evening for this, be sure to dedicate enough silent and undisturbed time for yourself in which you will be able to read the materials and do the practical parts. Take it one

---

[23] There is increasing evidence that physical activity has significant positive effects on the brain; among other things, physical activity impacts our learning and memory. Henriette van Praag, "Exercise and the Brain: Something to Chew On", *Trends Neurosci*, 32 (2009), 283-290. Physically being in nature is immensely restorative, but interestingly enough, Berto's study found that photographs of nature were also effective. Participants did two tests that required sustained attention with a break in between. During their break, those who looked at photographs of nature (as opposed to urban ones or geometric shapes) did significantly better on the test that followed the break than the other two groups. So even a picture of a relaxing beach, a mountain or forest will help if you do not manage to get out for your every break. Rita Berto, "Exposure to Restorative Environments Helps Restore Attentional Capacity", *Journal of Environmental Psychology*, Vol. 25 (2005), 249-259.

[24] Studies have shown that sleeping enough, and at the right times, is crucial to our overall health; those who disrupt their biological rhythms are at a higher risk of developing a number of different types of cancer. David E. Blask, "Melatonin, Sleep Disturbance and Cancer Risk", *Sleep Medicine Reviews*, 13 (2009), 257-264.

day at a time, as it is written, and resist the urge to hurry ahead and do more than you are assigned. Remember: the *process* is important, one day will be sufficient, trust this.

I wish you the very best as you prepare for your journey. Tomorrow you will begin...

DAY 1

the little man in the eye

«He found him in a desert land, and in a desolate, howling wilderness. He surrounded him on every side, He instructed him, He kept him as the apple of His eye.» Deuteronomy 32:10

Have you ever talked to someone who stood so close they were spitting on you? Did you find yourself slowly taking a step back because they were just too close for comfort? In the 1960 anthropologist Edward T. Hall studied the distances at which individuals interact and discovered four domains of interaction. They range from the public domain (the distance between the people is from 4m/12ft to more than 8m/25ft) to the intimate sphere (the distance being 45cm/18 inches or even less, depending on the circumstances).[25]

In this Hebrew passage, the phrase "the apple of His eye" literally means *'the little man in the eye'*. When most of us think of God, we think of Him as being far removed and uninterested in our lives. This passage

---

[25] 1) Intimate (15-50cm/0 – 6-18 inches) – The presence of the other person is unmistakable and may at times be overwhelming because of the greatly increased sensory inputs. This is the distance of lovemaking, wrestling, comforting and protecting. Physical contact, or its possibility, is uppermost in the awareness of both persons.

2) Personal (50-80cm/1.5-2.5ft) – At this distance one can hold or grasp the other person and the three-dimensional quality of objects is particularly pronounced. To keep someone at 'arms' length' is one way of expressing this domain. The voice level is moderate and no body heat is perceptible.

3) Social (1.20-2, 2-3.5m/4-7, 7-12ft) – Intimate visual details of the face are not perceived and nobody touches or expects to touch another person unless there is some special effort. Voice level is considered normal and conversations at this level can be overheard up to 6m/20ft.

4) Public (3.5-7.5, 7.5<m/12-25, 25<ft) – The voice is loud but not full volume. At 4m/16ft the body begins to lose its roundness and looks flat. The colour of the eyes is indiscernible, only the white of the eyes is visible. Much of the nonverbal part of the communication shifts to gestures and body stance. The tempo of the voice drops and words are enunciated more clearly. Generally, the whole person is seen as quite small and is perceived in a setting. Edward T. Hall, *Proxemics: the study of man's spatial relations,* (Unknown binding, 1962).

is attempting to break down that misconception by conveying the exact opposite. This text says that God is *always* so close to you that if you were to look into His eyes, you would see your entire reflection in His eyes.

Do you feel that God is distant and uninterested in your life? Have you ever felt that He was close to you or you were close to Him?

Imagine yourself and God as shapes then draw the two of you on a piece of paper. Do not *try* to be creative and do not give yourself time to think about what you are going to draw. Simply pick the colours that first come to you and draw.

«As one taps into creative flow, there are no mistakes, only new possibilities.»[26]

*   *   *

Take a look at your drawing...

Which colours did you use?

Do these colours remind you of anything? (Writing down your associations will make further analysis easier as you will not have to memorise them all. For example, associations can be memories, seeing a certain thing or place in your mind, suddenly thinking of something you recently read or heard, a sensation or idea, etc.)

Take a look at the shapes – what are they like?

Are they similar, different?

Are they the same size, is one larger or smaller?

What do you look like?

What does God look like?

Looking at the entire paper, are the shapes small in comparison to the page, or do they fill the entire space?

Are they in the middle, off to the side?

What is the distance between them?

Would you say they were close to each other or further apart?

---

[26] Mitchell S. Kossak, "Therapeutic Attunement: A Transpersonal View of Expressive Arts Therapy, *The Arts in Psychotherapy*, 36 (2009) 13-18.

Which of Hall's four domains would they fall into?

What might this drawing be telling you about your interaction with God?

Is there anything else it might be revealing?

Reflect on the times you felt you and God were close. Note them down and notice if there is a common thread between them. If you feel you have never been close to God, what might be the reason for it? Note down your thoughts and impressions.

How do you feel when reflecting on the realisation from the passage that God is so close to you?

What thoughts does it inspire?

What reaction does it elicit from you?

In the designated space in your notebook, you may want to write out your thoughts, a prayer or any additional impressions reflecting what you have contemplated today.

Day 2

«He found him in a desert land, and in a desolate, howling wilderness. He surrounded him on every side, He instructed him, He kept him as the apple of His eye.» Deuteronomy 32:10

It is the same passage as yesterday, but today the focus is on the other part of the text. There are four verbs that are ascribed to God. They are referring to His people – the Israelites referred to here in the singular as Jacob – and He is described as someone who takes care of them in different ways. If we were to personalise it, then it would mean that He:

1. *finds you* (in Hebrew this word means to discover, to uncover something)
2. *surrounds you* (it means to go around, to engulf, and in this particular tense, it means to *change*)
3. *instructs you* (to understand, to care, to discern, realise, have a skill/ insight, explain)
4. *keeps you* (to guard, watch, keep, protect, preserve)

God is always searching for you and can find you wherever you may be. From yesterday you already know that as far as He is concerned, He is always close to you, ready, willing and able. If you allow yourself to be found by Him, He begins to change you. This verb is used in a tense that means *'to busy oneself eagerly with the action in question'.* Plainly said, in this context God excitedly and very actively begins to change and transform you. Not only that, but He genuinely cares about you, so He advises you and explains things to you… He always understands you.

All four of these verbs are written in tenses that clearly indicate that these actions are incomplete, ongoing, progressive and actively being taken care of.

* Keep this in mind: *even when God seems passive, distant and silent, He is diligently and faithfully going about His business with you.*

Without thinking about it, which one of these four actions appeals to you, speaks to you most? Depict the one that seems to call out to you most strongly in a drawing.

*   *   *

Looking at your drawing, what do you see?
Which colours did you use?
Did you use many or a few?
What is the story behind what you have drawn?
Is your drawing more abstract or concrete?
Does it remind you of anything (as a whole or part of it)?

Notice which one of the four actions you chose as your main one, the one you have drawn. Why might this one be the most important to you?

Is this something you often experience, or would you perhaps like to experience it more often?

Can you recall any times when you felt God was e.g. guarding you, protecting you?

If so, when was the last time you felt that way?

Of which other three actions would you like to be more aware?

How might you be able to bring about that greater awareness?

Your prayer:

DAY 3
truth => freedom

«Then Jesus said to the Jews who believed Him, "If you continue to be in My word, you are truly My disciples; and you will come to know the truth, and the truth will make you free."» John 8:32

Have you ever bought anything online? If the answer is yes, when was the last time and what did you buy? In 2016 global e-commerce sales (from businesses to customers) were expected to reach 1.92 trillion \$US.[27] According to these statistics, in 2013 there were 191.1 million digital shoppers in the America alone and that figure was projected to surpass 200 million in 2015. In 2015, e-retail sales accounted for 7.4% of all retail sales worldwide. This figure is expected to reach 13% in 2019.

Whether you are from Los Angeles or London, have you ever bought something online and then eagerly waited for it to arrive? I like to buy books and just knowing that I will soon have in my hands what I have eagerly wanted to read is so exciting. Today's passage talks of a similar experience.

There are many ways we could understand or conceptualise the 'truth', and throughout history there have been many different ways in which this concept has been understood. The Western world has been greatly shaped by the classical Greek cultural heritage, including its general understanding of the notion of truth.

'To know' (γινώσκω) in Greek means to learn something, to find out, it is the notion of something coming together and forming a larger picture.

One way in which the truth can be understood from a Greek point of view is truth as 'that which is'; truth is that which is unveiled, revealed, that which is to be clearly seen. While that is one way of looking at it, if we turn to the ancient Israelites and their understanding we find another perspective of 'truth'. Consider the following passage:

"The faithfulness of God is the truth that must be told. It is no logical

---

[27] http://www.statista.com/topics/871/online-shopping/

43

universal. It is not a philosophical category. As truth it is deeply personal [...] The divine truth is a relation into which every man can enter. By the same token it is a relation from which man can turn – a truth which they can lose. To 'lose' the truth is to forget God [...] Truth for the Old Testament is never an ultimate universal comprehending all existence within itself; it is always the experienced faithfulness of God as the Holy One: creative, law-giving, judging, redemptive. Though not itself a logical universal, it illuminates all existence [...]"[28]

Author Edward Ramsdell touches the heart of the ancient Israelite understanding of the truth when he highlights the relational, personal and experiential element of it. Today we tend to think of truth as information and fact, as an abstract proposition, but this view was radically different and particularly engaging. If truth was a relationship for the ancient Israelites, then the way in which a person could enter into that relationship was in the following way:

«It [the truth] is apprehended in the response of faith [...] It involves the life of the believer, his personal commitment and self-surrender. Yet it is no matter of blind allegiance. Faith witnesses to the faithfulness of God. What God has done for Israel can be told and what He promises can be experienced. In the light of that faithfulness every man can understand himself and his common life. He can 'walk' in God's truth and find his way illuminated.»[29]

In the ancient biblical view, truth is a relationship, the experience of God's faithfulness and a response of faithfulness to Him.

This understanding of truth as a relationship is not just confined to the Hebrew Bible, we also find other Bible passages that speak of the same concept (Jesus says that He is 'the Way, the Truth and the Life', John 14:6). With all of this in mind, when you consider today's text and the truth setting you free, it implies that it is not an idea or set of propositions that will change you, but it is the Truth Himself who will free you.

---

[28] Edward T. Ramsdell, "The Old Testament Understanding of Truth", *The Journal of Religion* Vol. 31 (1951), 264-273, esp. 271, 272.
[29] Ramsdell, "The Old Testament Understanding of Truth", 272.

It is not some*thing* that frees you, it is some*one*, God. The key component is the *connection* with Him.

In this passage the Greek verb meaning 'to set free' is in a tense called the *future active indicative*. The fascinating thing about this tense is that it is used to portray something that is going to take place in the future in the following way: it is *the present vividly projected into the future*.

In other words it is your reality today, it is something that belongs in the present but has been moved up into the future. It is much like buying that special something online – you have paid for it, you are simply waiting for it to arrive, but it is already yours and it *will* arrive.

Be encouraged – perhaps what you have asked of God you have *already received*, you might just have to wait a little longer to feel its full effect. Remember, He is close and busy working in and around you, and He will free you.

Draw a line down the middle of a piece of paper that you will use to draw on. On the left side draw yourself as 'captive' and on the right side of the paper draw yourself as 'free'.

*   *   *

Take your paper into your hands and notice what you have drawn...

To which half of the page are you initially drawn to? Why?

How did you find the task of drawing them, was it easy, difficult?

Was one easier than the other? If so, which one?

Is what you have drawn two separate drawings or one that progresses into the other? What colours have you used, similar for both or do they differ?

Without thinking, if your 'captive' drawing were a sound, what would it be?

And if your 'free' drawing were a sound, what would it be?

What do you notice about those sounds? Do they conjure any associations or memories?

Having explored the image from multiple angles (using various senses in your imagination), do you find it gives you a fuller grasp of the images you have drawn?

Belinda É. Samari

A closing quote for today:

«The faithfulness of God is the ultimate apprehension. He is the absolutely firm (as the root idea of *emeth* suggests), the unfailingly dependable, the eternally trustworthy. YHVH's faithfulness is His eternal character. It stands in contrast to all change, to all that is ephemeral, to all that is local and particular [...] In all this there is, of course, no interest in any philosophical definition of truth; but, the moment YHVH appears as the true God in contrast to false gods, that moment the Hebrew mind had a notion of absolute truth.»[30]

Your prayer:

---

[30] Ramsdell, "The Old Testament Understanding of Truth", 266, 267. In Biblical Hebrew the letters YHVH (also seen as YHWH) designate the name of God; there is a long history regarding how YHVH came to be translated as (capitalised) LORD in English, however that is not of interest at this point. Scholars are unsure how the name would have been pronounced (as the original Hebrew scrolls had no vowels, just consonants), but the most common examples are Yahveh or Yehova/Jehovah. In the Bible passages in this book I will use YHVH as whatever the pronunciation might have been, I find it is important to bear in mind that those letters are nevertheless a representation of God's name, thus I prefer its use over the impersonal LORD, which is not a name, but a title.

DAY 4
growth

«Wake up, wake up, put on your strength...» Isaiah 52:1

If people were meant to pop out of bed, we'd all sleep in toasters. ~ Author unknown, attributed to Jim Davis

At some point in our lives we have all woken up and experienced that moment – that moment you are abruptly pushed out of your dream world and slowly (or not so slowly) the realisation hits you that you now have to get up and dive into the waking hours that are staring you in the face. How we wake up in the morning can often influence our mood that entire day.

When talking of the mind and awareness in their book on God and the brain, Newberg, D'Acquili and Rause say the following:

«There seems to be, within the human head, an inner, personal awareness, a free-standing, observant self. We have come to think of this self, with all its emotions, sensations, and cognitions, as the phenomenon of *mind*. Neurology cannot completely explain how such a thing can happen – how a nonmaterial mind can rise from mere biological functions; how flesh and blood machinery of the brain can suddenly become 'aware'.»[31]

Being aware is a mysteriously wonderful phenomenon we experience and we cannot live our lives without it. Our level of awareness, whether in regard to ourselves or others, can vary throughout our lives and can be significantly increased. The greater the awareness, the greater and more meaningful our impact in the *milieu* we are in, and greater *awareness* is always linked to *growth*. Being awake is being aware, using our mind and intuition, our whole brain to the best of our ability in order to live well balanced and rounded lives. God says: wake up, put on your strength. Imagine 'strength' as an item of clothing you can put on each morning. Wake up, be alert, start being aware of yourself and of the things around

---

[31] Newberg, D'Acquili and Rause, *Why God Won't Go Away*, 32.

you. Get ready, what lies ahead will be unpleasant but it is necessary because that is how you grow.

«Growth is not a place at which ones arrives. It is not a goal. On the contrary, it is a long process of conjugation and dispersion… [growth] is a continuous transformational state of mind.»[32]

Many of us want to grow and become better people; we would like to advance and excel but not too many of us are ready to accept the pain that comes with it.

In the coming days why not resolve to be more aware and (begin to) embrace the idea that growth also involves unpleasant and painful moments. In this ongoing process you will progress in your awareness and become more like the person God envisioned you to be.

Go for a walk in your area and take with you a notepad and pen. If possible go to a place where you have not been before because new surroundings make it easier to form new pathways in your brain. As you walk, focus on one sense at a time and write down what you notice. You may choose to sit for a while, but do also move around because changing positions alters our perceptions of that to which we are exposed. Below are some examples to help you get into the creative flow – be free and as imaginative as you dare. Do this for each sense (sight, sound, touch, smell – except taste, unless you would like to sample the shrubs and lawns).

Sight – notice various shapes, sizes you can see, the nearest, furthest objects, the ones you like, the ones you do not like, the ones that intrigue you (if any), the ones that repel you, etc.

Sound – notice what you are hearing, notice to what you turn your attention and actually listen to, notice where the sounds are coming from, whether they are pleasant or unpleasant, sharp, dull, loud, aggravating, which sound is closest, note down any associations with the sounds you hear…[33]

Smell – notice how many different scents you can detect, where they

---

[32] Dario Sor and Senet de Gazzano (1993), as quoted in Leandro Stitzman, "At-one-ment, intuition and 'suchness'", *The International Journal of Psychoanalysis*, Vol. 85 (2004), 1137-1155, 1140.

[33] "Sound is […] all perceptible vibrations (sonic formations). The relationship of all perceptible sounds is important […] More often than not, urban living causes narrow

might be coming from, what kind of story might be linked to them, perhaps try to describe the various scents, or write down any associations you have with them...

Touch – notice the textures of the things you touch, how they compare, what they might remind you of, which ones appeal to you and which ones perhaps leave you indifferent, notice how they feel on your skin...[34]

*   *   *

Looking at the notes from your walk, what do you notice?

Is there anything that strikes you quite obviously?

In which sense (sight, sound etc.) was the observation the easiest? The most difficult? Which did you enjoy most? Note down anything that might come up as a result of reflecting on what you experienced.

If you were to take your experience outdoors and link it to the spiritual dimension, what observations might you make? Are there ways in which you could become more aware of God every day?

Your prayer:

---

focus and disconnection." Pauline Oliveros, *Deep Listening: A Composer's Sound Practice* (Lincoln, NE: Deep Listening Publications, 2005), xxiv, xxv.

[34] "Touch is the most personal of the senses. Hearing and touch meet where the lower frequencies of audible sound pass over to tactile vibrations (at about 20 hertz). Hearing is a way of touching at a distance." R. Murray Schafer, *Our Sonic Environment and the Soundscape and the Tuning of the World* (Rochester: Destiny Books, 1994), 11.

DAY 5
space & light

«But I am like a flourishing olive tree in the house of God; I trust in the kindness of God forever and ever.» Psalms 52:8[35]

Today the focus is on three concepts: space, light, and *chesed.*[36]

The olive tree is to the world of flora what the lion is to the jungle: the king. Olive trees have extensively spreading roots that extend around every tree in order to absorb sufficient moisture in the dry conditions in which they usually grow. It is because of this that they are usually planted approximately several metres apart so that they can spread and each tree receives enough space and light. These are the best conditions for bearing fruit: *space* and *light.* It is their elaborate root system that allows olive trees to tolerate drought so well. They can live exceptionally long (if correctly and regularly pruned) and they grow very slowly. In today's text the Psalmist says he is like a green olive tree in the house of God. The word green here means verdant, luxuriant, prosperous and flourishing. In essence he is saying that he is prospering and blossoming in God's presence.

God is the one who knows olive trees inside and out, who lovingly prunes them and tills the soil. He takes care of them and protects them from pests and diseases. He knows exactly when to harvest the drupes and how to extract as much oil and goodness from the fruit. He even knows how to put the entire fruit to use, including the leaves and pits. Because He knows all of this to the smallest detail not only about olive trees but also about you, being in His presence is good for you – you have ideal conditions in which to grow and you can survive even when things in life

---

[35] In the coming days the Psalms will feature often, so I am grateful to Dr Laurence Turner for drawing my attention to Walter Brueggemann's framework that might be of interest to you: Psalms of orientation-disorientation-reorientation. For more information see Walter Brueggemann, *The Message of the Psalms: A Theological Commentary,* (Minneapolis: Fortress Press, 1985).
[36] The 'ch' is pronounced as a deep, throaty 'h'.

do not go smoothly, when you are challenged and find yourself in harsh, painful circumstances.

If you allow yourself to be planted in His olive grove, with the right amount of space and light, the rest will follow.

Today you will have two smaller tasks, one is to mind map and the other is to draw something.

Make two mind maps in the shape of a tree, one for 'space' and the other for 'light'. Off the top of your head, without stopping to think, scribble down words, phrases or even symbols that spring to mind when you consider these two things. For the purpose of today's exercise, make your mind maps by way of association. For example, 'table' – wood, strong, sturdy, four legs, eat, people, together… Like beads on a shoestring, one word creates an association of another and that one of another and so it goes. In this case, space and light are the initial trigger words that will help you to unravel your associations.

*   *   *

Have a look at your maps…

Which one has more branches?

Which one flowed easiest? Do you know why?

Is there any similarity between them?

How are they different?

Is there anything on your maps that jumps out at you? If so, be free to explore it…

Do you have enough space in your life at the moment?

Are you getting enough light?

Are you perhaps planted too near some other trees and feel crowded?

Or perhaps the opposite, are you on the verge of isolation?

David says he trusts in God's *chesed*, His loyalty, mercy and unfailing love, His devotion and kindness. *Chesed* is typically deemed to be an act that has no cause. It is seen as proactive, as the primary spark that initiates subsequent action. In other words, the way God loves us does not depend on how much we love Him, how devoted we are to Him, how much time we spend with Him… He loves us because it is who He is – He is kind and loyal to us regardless of how we are to Him. He is Love. This gives

David the strength and encouragement he needs, knowing God will never fail him. Ever. [37]

Have you thought about love as proactive, regardless of how others are towards you? How do you feel about God's *chesed* towards you? What might be some ways in which you could practically begin to adopt this proactive attitude in your daily life?

If you were a tree what would you be like? Draw what you see in your imagination...

*　　　*　　　*

What kind of tree are you?

What associations come to mind when you look at your tree?

Where are you planted? What is the setting?

What is the landscape like that surrounds you?

Does this tree bear any resemblance to a tree(s) from your real life experience at any stage? Does it carry any meaning for you?

If this tree could speak, what would it say? Note down any impressions...

What is this drawing telling you about yourself?

Does it bring up associations in regard to anything else? Write down all of your observations and perhaps come back to them if and whenever you feel the need to.

Your prayer:

---

[37] "It is clear that [*chesed*] is a relational concept [...] three elements constitutive of the *chesed* concept: it is active, social and enduring [...] [it] always designates not just a human attitude, but also the act that emerges from this attitude. It is an act that preserves and promotes life. It is an intervention on behalf of someone who is suffering misfortune or distress. It is demonstration of friendship [...] The concept lies within the realm of interpersonal relations [...] wife and husband, father and son, host and guest, relatives, friends, and those who have formed a relationship based on unexpected acts of kindness [...] the one who receives an act of *chesed* responds with a similar act of *chesed*, or at least that the one who demonstrates *chesed* is justified in expecting an equivalent act in return [...]" G. Johannes Botterweck and Helmer Ringgren, "Chesed", *Theological Dictionary of the Old Testament*, Vol.V, (Grand Rapids, MI: Wm. B. Eerdmans Publishing Company, 1986), 47, 49, 51.

DAY 6
wholeness

«Bless YHVH, oh my soul, and do not forget all His rewards; who forgives all your sins, heals all your diseases [...]» Psalms 103:2-3

We often associate healing with the disappearance of an illness, the illness seen as the enemy that is to be fought and destroyed. Yet in his article on wholeness and healing Jeremy Swayne suggests that the essential characteristic of healing is that it is creative, and not just remedial. He mentions a general principle of healing that may seem counterintuitive at first, but one that I find has some validity. Rather than suffering from an illness, he says, we are often suffering from a 'wellness'.[38] Just as hunger is the response of a healthy body to the lack of food, so the pain of rejection, abuse, the denial of love and of self worth is the healthy response of our wounded humanity because we are denied some quality of life (that we need) that is fundamental to the fulfillment of our unique potential as a person.

He continues by saying that healing cannot be achieved without suffering because illness is the agent of healing. In other words, the challenge and the discomfort we experience whether mentally or emotionally is often crucial in order for us to develop new insights and strengths.[39]

This passage in the Psalms mentions healing and, much like Jeremy Swayne's view, it represents a more 'whole' concept. The Hebrew word

---

[38] He also lays out some general and fundamental principles that govern the healing process. For example, Swayne states that in one way or another all healing involves the following elements – understanding the problem, providing the conditions that will facilitate healing, mobilising the resources to effect healing, new growth, and reconciliation. Jeremy Swayne, "Homeopathy, Wholeness and Healing", *Homeopathy* 94 (2005), 37-42.

[39] "Pain is the tool our cells use to communicate to our brain that there is trauma somewhere in the body. Our cells stimulate our pain receptors in order to get our brain to focus and pay attention. Once the brain acknowledges the existence of the pain then it has served its purpose and either lightens up in intensity, or goes away." Bolte Taylor, *My Stroke of Insight*, 157.

'to heal' (*rapha*, רָפָא) means *to make whole*, to go from unclean to clean, defective to complete.

«God speaks to the intellect and feelings both at the same time [...] It is certain that God did not intend that man should be torn apart by the contradictions of his nature, but that he should be an integrated being [...] The only hope of reconciling the warring aspects of human nature is through faith in the One in whom all opposites coincide.»[40]

This idea of a human being as a whole is fundamental from a Biblical perspective. True healing is deep and thorough and it takes into account the bigger picture. We know from personal experience that for any complex structure to function well, whether the VW factory in Dresden or the human body, all of its components need to work in harmony. What we eat, drink, do, think and feel either helps or hinders us from leading more meaningful and fulfilling lives.

Copy the matrix of squares into the journal you are using alongside this book. Once you have done that, with your colouring pencils or crayons, fill in each square as you wish (e.g. drawing, colouring, writing), each one representing a part of you. These 'parts' could be roles you have (e.g. mother, student, brother-in-law) or they could be a prominent physical feature you identify with for whatever reason (e.g. my big nose), adjectives you strongly identify with (e.g. creative, organised), your profession (e.g. dentist), or any other aspect of yourself... You can label the parts on the back side of the paper if you like. These are just intended as guides; the key is to not think about it but simply go along and fill in the squares one by one... You may find you will only fill in a few squares rather than all twelve, or you may find you need more. Again, this grid is intended merely as a guide and the number will differ from person to person, so fill in as many as feels right for you...

---

[40] Johann W. Göthe, *Aus Meinem Leben: Dichtung und Wahrheit*, book 12.

*   *   *

Now that you have completed your work, reflect on each part of you (your squares) and note down any associations you have with each part.

*   *   *

When you have done this for all the parts, turn your paper over and notice your labels, their interrelations, which part is next to which, which parts are on the farthest ends, etc., notice if this arrangement of your parts evokes any observations...

Which colours did you use for which parts, are there any similarities between them? What are your associations with the colours you used?

Are there any connections between these colours and those in your previous drawings?

How long have you 'had' any of these parts of yourself?

Which one is the oldest, which one the newest?

How did you come to acquire them in the first place?

Of your own choosing or through some other circumstances?

Which part of yourself is your favourite?

And your least favourite?

Which one would you like to change? Why?

When you reflect on your parts, where would you say they are on the scale from harmonious to disharmonious?

Are there any 'diseases' you recognise from which you might need or want healing?

I once read a quote that said: Pain is inevitable, suffering is optional.

If you could narrow it down, what seems to be the main reason for your suffering?

On the next blank page in your notebook, fill the entire space of the page as you like - in contrast to the parts of yourself which are disparate, perhaps conflicting and unbalanced, this space now represents the whole of you, not as a sum of fragments but as an integrated whole...

*   *   *

Consider your 'whole' self as you have drawn it...

How does your 'whole' differ from your 'parts'?

How is it similar?

What do you first notice about it?

What emotions does it stir up?

Ask yourself the same questions as you did for your 'parts' (those that apply)...

Let your mind wander and if there are any questions of your own that seem to be coming through, make note of them and feel free to explore them...

In practical terms, what could you do to make it easier for God to heal you, what can you do to contribute to the healing process from your side?

Your prayer:

DAY 7
your innermost part

«*I will bless YHVH, who counsels me; even at night my heart instructs me.*»
Psalms 16:7

Did you know that your whole brain does not fall asleep at the same time? In 2008, psychologists Maria Casagrande & Mario Bertini revealed that, to a certain degree, the LH is more active during the daytime and the RH more active during the night-time.[41] In addition to that they discovered that as we fall asleep, our LH falls asleep first. Bearing in mind the creative and imaginative characteristics of the RH, this seems to echo what was mentioned in the Psalms long ago.

In Psalms 16:7 David says that at night his heart instructs him. Usually the Hebrew word *lev* (לֵב) is what is most often translated as 'heart' in English. However, the term translated as 'heart' here literally means 'kidney', *kilyah* (כִּלְיָה).[42] It differs from *lev* in that it often represents the

---

[41] Maria Casagrande and Mario Bertini, "Laterality of the sleep onset process: Which hemisphere goes to sleep first?", *Biological Psychology* 77, no. 1 (2008), 76-80. Maria Casagrande and Mario Bertini, "Night-time right hemisphere superiority and daytime left hemisphere superiority: A repatterning of laterality across wake-sleep-wake states", *Biological Psychology* 77, no. 3 (2008), 337-342. Even during the day the cycle of hemispherical activity is regulated approximately every 90 minutes. The hemispheres alternate in phases in which one will be more dominant, and then they switch and do so throughout the day. Eric Jensen, *Brain-Based Learning*, (Thousand Oaks, California: Corwin Press, 2000), 26.

[42] There are a few Hebrew words that are translated as the English 'heart' but their meaning is nuanced. In the case of these two terms, *lev* is literally the organ that pumps blood, but was not used literally but rather metaphorically, what we would today call the 'mind'; *lev* was understood as the centre of a person's being, the seat of thought, emotion, intention, plans, etc. When *kilyah* is used as the 'heart', it emphasises the inner self and Dr Garabed Eknoyan points out the analogy to how deeply the kidneys are physically encased in fat. Garabed Eknoyan, "The Kidneys in the Bible: What Happened?", *Journal of the American Society of Nephrology*, 16 (2005), 3464-71. An example of the use of both terms in the same passage (Ps. 26:2: 'Examine me, O YHVH, try me; test my kidneys (*kilyah*) and my heart (*lev*).' (my translation)

innermost place of the human being, emphasising this organ as our inner self, like a kernel of wheat; the innermost layer possible.[43]

In the still of the night David was aware of his communication with God,[44] it was an exchange in which God was teaching him, giving him advice and guidance. He was also pointing out where David was a little off the mark and to what he needed to pay more attention. Like two friends with walkie-talkies – if they are not on the same frequency, nothing they say will get through to the other person and their communication will be pointless, to say the least. In the same way, if our innermost self is in tune with God then our communication is meaningful. As a result, it fills our daily lives with purpose. This account is not an exception, something that only David experienced, but an example of what is available to each of us.

Imagine yourself as having many layers (like an onion). As it usually is, not everyone you interact with has access to all of your layers. But imagine you are now peeling them back, layer by layer… Finally you get deep within and cannot go any further - there it lies, the deepest place within you, the very core of your being. This is your inner self that only God knows and sees, the part of you He communicates with and to which He connects. What is this innermost part of you like? Draw what you see in your imagination…

*   *   *

Have a look at your artwork… What do you see?
If you were to give it a title or a name, what would it be?
Why?
How would you describe your innermost part?
If you were to compare it to something, what would it be?
Of what does it remind you?
Comfortably quiet, sit with what you have drawn and notice what associations come to mind. Write them down and do not analyse them,

---

[43] The research for my MA dissertation on human body parts in the Hebrew Bible revealed that the kidneys are also often the seat of deep pain (Job 16:13; 19:27, Lam. 3:13, Ps. 73:21).

[44] Among others, here are a few texts that also reveal elements of RH activity at nighttime: Ps. 42:8; 63:6; 77:6.

simply notice and write them down. When you have done this and are ready to move on, take a look at what you have written down. Now apply a LH Sherlock Holmes-like attitude and notice whether there are any connections between your associations, if any kind of bigger picture emerges...

Somehow God has access to the innermost part of you where no one else can go. It reminds me of those private dining rooms sometimes found in restaurants or a VIP section in an establishment. You meet with God in that private room for leisurely discussions, to listen and debate, to share dreams of the future, for storytelling and advice. Why not use your VIP pass?

Among other things, as we saw our linear and analytical self falls asleep first leaving our more 'whole', intuitive and imaginative self awake for a while longer.

Taking fuller advantage of that discovery, tonight when you are in bed, relaxed and ready to sleep, close your eyes and bring yourself to a state of quietness. Lie in a comfortable position and notice if any images come to mind (it might help to imagine a big blank screen on which something might appear). The first time you do this nothing may seem to surface, but if you continue to do this regularly, you will begin to notice images surfacing more easily. Once they do, notice what they are, retain them in your memory and in the morning, draw them or write down a description of them that will help you remember and then reflect on them when you have some quiet time. These images can be highly effective in 'translating' internal content in a visual way that is comprehensible (an image really does speak a thousand words).[45]

---

[45] "Images play a key role in some forms of reasoning, if only as 'mental notepads,' helping one to keep track of the things being reasoned about and the relations among them. However, it is clear that images alone cannot support reasoning. Images must be 'under description': any given image could have an infinite number of meanings (e.g., an apple could stand for an apple, fruit, food for worms, motherhood, etc.), and yet we are not confused about what we are thinking about when we have an image. The image must be interpreted by processes that themselves are not ambiguous. Hence, the role of imagery in reasoning must be understood within the context of a larger processing system, which also makes use of propositional representations." S. J. Stose and S. M. Kosslyn, "Imagery versus Propositional Reasoning" in *The International Encyclopedia of the Social & Behavioral Sciences*, eds. James D. Wright, Neil J. Smelser and Paul B. Baltes, (Elsevier Science Ltd, 2001), 7193-7197, 7196.

Belinda É. Samari

Your prayer:

So it is with the images that surface from within, though we might initially be confused about their meaning, somehow we *do* know what they stand for – if nothing else, we know what they *do not* stand for – until we become aware of their true meaning.

DAY 8
hope

«For there is hope for a tree, if it is cut down, that it will sprout again, and that its tender shoot will not cease. Though its root may grow old in the earth, and its stump may die in the ground, yet at the scent of water it will bud and bring forth branches like a plant.»
Job 14:7-9

Often concepts such as love, wonder, courage and hope are difficult to define, stuck in an abstract sphere that prevents us from adequately expressing their essence. As you may have noticed already, Hebrew is a language embedded with images and its abstract concepts are entrenched in a poetic concreteness.

'Hope' is *tiqvah* (תִּקְוָה) and in Hebrew each word is based on a root of three letters.[46] In this case, *tiqvah* is derived from the root QVH (קָוָה) meaning 'to wait'. The word 'hope' is, so to speak, built on the word 'to wait'; the two are closely intertwined.

Imagine your heart and mind as this tree in the text. Even if you are repeatedly being sabotaged and destroyed, if you keep failing and perhaps even self-destructing in one way or another – that does not have to be the final verdict on you as a person or your life. You can change and move forward, you can grow (ever so tenderly, one step at a time) and spring up slowly.

Even if the very essence dies, even if all the roots you have spread out wither and die, it only takes one whiff of His presence, just a smidgen of your awareness of Him and His Spirit and you will bloom. You will spread again and fly, spreading your wings like the eagle you are and always were supposed

---

[46] To make this concept a little clearer, one such root is **MLK** meaning to reign, to be or become king/queen. The root letters are in bold. Words derived from this root are for example: **melekh** (king), **malki** (my king), **malkah** (queen), **mamlakhah** (kingdom)… As you can see, the root is always present in any word, and the individual words are formed by inserting vowels in certain ways that subsequently make them adjectives, nouns, adverbs, etc.

to be. *No matter how many times you get stuck and give up on yourself, on ideas, on others, the message from this tree is simple: there is a way and there is hope. All you need is to come closer to Him and then watch Him transform you and your life.*

* Remember: things that are of lasting value come slowly (the *process* is the essence of *progress*).

Imagine that tree that is withered, dry and for all intents and purposes deemed dead and useless. Yet against all odds, at one moment in time it begins to bloom again and keeps on growing and flourishing. Freely using your imagination, write a story about this tree and its journey from its most miserable state to its flourishing revival (weave in the themes of hope and waiting). Do not worry about what you will write, simply begin your story with the words

«Once upon a time there was a tree...»

and go where it takes you. After you have finished your story, sit with it for a while and let it sink in...

*   *   *

After some time of contemplation and silence, what have you noticed?

Was there something(s) that was immediately obvious to you about the story?

Was there anything that surprised you, puzzled you?

Is there anything you dislike? If so, what is it and why might that be the case?

Does your tree remind you of anything?

Are there any aspects of the story (the tree's journey or others) that resonate with you?

Are there any similarities with any of the previous exercises you have done so far? Emerging patterns are most often significant...

How were the motifs of hope and waiting threaded into your story?

Are these or any other motifs ones you can identify in your own life?

What insight can you draw from this? It may be an idea, a sentence, even a word or an image... Note it down and come back to it whenever you get tired of waiting and need a reminder of this withered tree that slowly came to life again.

Your prayer:

DAY 9

trust => discovery

«Enable me to hear of Your love (chesed) in the morning, because I rely on You. Make me know the way I should walk, for I lift up my self to You.»
Psalms 143:8

Are you a morning person? An early bird up and about while the night owls are still snoozing? On DAY 7 the focus was on the RH and its activity during the night-time whereas today our attention turns to the morning hours of the day.

Dawn is a welcome change after the night-time, the moment when the residue of the night melts away into the awakening of a new day. It is a kind of border, a liminal time and space of transition filled with exciting new beginnings and unknown opportunities. The daytime is a time to *live* that which you have accumulated and become aware of during the night in your time of quiet contemplation.

When a new day begins, David asks to discern and experience God's *chesed* (see DAY 5 for a reminder) in the morning. He asks for God's advice on which paths to take, he actively sets aside time so that he can attentively listen to God's input on what is on his 'agenda' for that day, and then take it on board as he heads out into the day.

The literal meaning of trust in this text is: *'to hide for refuge'*.[47] In the time of ancient Israel there were cities designated as safe havens for all those who had broken a law and needed protection. If you reached one of these cities before your enemies caught up with you, they had no right to harm you and you were safe. Bearing that in mind, how does 'to hide for refuge' relate to 'trust'? Before moving on, let this image sink in a little...

* *God is your ultimate safe haven in every sense of the word.*[48]

---

[47] *Batach,* בָּטַח
[48] Proverbs 18:10

64

First impressions tend to mean a lot and we often judge whether a person is trustworthy or not within roughly thirty seconds upon meeting them, though most often the true test is that of time. We can trust complete strangers if the situation calls for it, but in most cases trust is something found between those who know each other well. Without trust no friendship or relationship can exist or progress.

It is only with this absolute, unwavering trust in God's goodness towards us that we can even proceed to the next step, to discern the path in which He wants us to walk.

The idea of hearing God in Hebrew also means much more than to simply hear. It means 'to hear intelligently,' meaning you are not only hearing, but you are listening because you want to engage with that which you are hearing. You are listening because you want what you are hearing to shape your actions from that moment onwards. You listen to something and understand it, and then you go and *live it.*

Flip back through the days leading up to today. What have you learnt (perhaps jot down the basic ideas)? How does the notion of trusting (or beginning to trust) God seem after what you have learnt so far?

As stated, one of the images in Hebrew for trust is 'to hide for refuge'. What would your image of 'trust' be? What is the first thing that springs to mind?

Exercises like the one you are about to do are usually read aloud by someone while you would have your eyes closed and could delve into your imagination. Since that might not be possible, I have written it out in such a way that you can read one sentence at a time, imagine it, then when you are ready, open your eyes and read the next line. Or, if possible, read through the whole thing memorising the sequence and then with eyes closed, imagine the whole story. Whatever you choose, there is no rush at all so immerse yourself in the imagery by giving yourself time to really experience each segment of the story at your own pace.

Find a quiet place where you can sit or lie down. Ensure you will not be disturbed and you will be able to relax. Do your best to quiet your inner chatter and any distracting thoughts.

Imagine you are in a luscious green jungle...

To either side of you are tall trees with beautiful foliage...

You can hear the chirping of the tropical birds...

You can feel the rays of sunshine warming you as they filter through the leaves of the trees...

You have been walking through the jungle for a long time...

You are searching for something...

You seem to have lost your sense of direction...

You want to go on but you are not sure which way to go...

You hear the rustling of leaves and turn to look...

Out from amongst the trees appears a wise person...

The person offers to help you find what you are looking for...

You follow the wise person walking closely behind...

After what seems like a long time, the wise person points straight ahead...

You walk a little way further on your own and suddenly come to a clearing...

You take a look around... What do you see?

When you feel you have been in your imagination long enough, slowly bring your attention back to the room before moving on.

*　　　*　　　*

Draw, scribble or write down the key elements of your story. To help you get started, How was it being in the jungle?

What were you looking for?

What was the wise person like? How would you describe your interaction?

How was it following the wise person to the place you were looking for?

What did you encounter when you reached the clearing?

How did you feel when you finally got there?

Note down anything else you find relevant to your story.

*　　　*　　　*

Today's text highlights how *trust leads to discovery*. David entrusted himself to God each morning and that, in turn, led him to discover the paths that were best for him to take.

Consider these two elements in your experience in the jungle. Take a look at your notes on the wise person – what is your description like? How did you feel at the proposition of the wise person offering to help lead you to your 'destination'? Were you curious, trusting, relieved, sceptical, anxious, _____?[49] Notice everything you wrote down in relation to the wise person and your interaction with him/her. How might your notes reflect your perception of God and your interaction with Him?

Whether you are familiar with God and already trust Him or are perhaps just slowly getting to know Him, consider how your level of trust impacts your daily life. Would you like to trust Him more? If so, what would help bring about that change?

Your prayer:

---

[49] 'Feel' can refer to your intuition, and also to your emotions, so consider both aspects when asked how you feel about something. In regard to 'feeling' as emotion, see the index at the back of the book for a long list of emotions that might help you more precisely articulate and express yourself. In general when I say 'feel' in the book, I am referring to the whole of your awareness of what is going on within, which includes intuition, emotion, thoughts, etc.

DAY 10

waiting

«Happy is the person who listens to Me, watching daily at My gates, waiting at the posts of My door. For whoever finds Me, finds life, and obtains favour from YHVH.» Proverbs 8:34-35

Copy the passage above into your notebook. Now read through the text again (this time aloud) and without thinking too much, circle the word/s that catch your attention and jump out at you.

Once you have done that, focus on the word/s you have circled and simply sit and listen... What floats to the surface? Imagine sitting at the bottom of a pool. If you allow yourself to simply be still, if you do not purposely move, you will slowly begin to float to the surface. When I say 'simply sit and listen' I mean do just that – as you would in a pool, allow yourself to be still and notice what floats to the surface of your awareness.

*   *   *

Happy. Listen. Watch. Wait. Find. Life. Favour.
Consider this:
If you are already waiting for something, why not wait on God?
If you want to find something, why not find God, the source of life?
If you want your problems solved, why not have Jesus take care of them (who can not only free you, but *create* new things in and around you)?
If you spend time on something, why not spend it on something that is of true worth, something that exceeds the here and now in its substance and value? Time is precious.
The essence of the text might be summarised as follows.

If you attentively listen for God's voice, if you wait at His door every day, it will *open. You will draw illumination from there, it will free you, because whoever finds God finds the very essence and source of life. Finding is a discovery, a process and a meeting. Once that occurs, you can be sure that God is pleased with you, that He is smiling at you and you are a delight in His eyes. Your debt will be taken care of, God approves of who you are and what you do.*

* It pays to wait at the right door every day.

As you did yesterday in your imaginative exercise, get yourself in a comfortable position and a place of quiet before continuing. When you are ready, gently close your eyes and imagine the following:

You are on a train...

You hear the rhythmic racket of the train on the railroad tracks...

The train is slowing down... You get up to leave...

The train comes to a complete halt and the doors open...

You step onto the platform... You are the only one that gets off the train...

The station is empty, there is no one around...

What you see before you is a large wall with many doors in it...

Notice what they look like...

You observe them carefully...

You notice each one has a sign on it, a label of some sort...

You realise that to go beyond the wall you must pass through one of the doors...

You slowly approach one...

As you get closer you can identify the sign...

How does it look…?

The door opens and you slowly step through... What do you see?

*   *   *

Note down what you experienced in your imagination. Answer questions along the lines of (but not necessarily restricted to) the following, also answering any of your own questions that may surface.

How would describe your experience of being on the train?

Do you know where you were headed?

What did the station look like when you stepped off the train?

What time of day/year was it?

How were you dressed?

How did you feel?

How many doors were there?

What did they look like, how would you describe them?

Could you see the signs on all the doors? If so, what were they like?

What was the sign like on the door you went through?

Was it a word, letters, or a symbol, what did it look like?

How did you feel about going through the door?

What drew you to that one in particular?

Once you passed through, where did it lead you?

Is there any resonance between what you saw and your real life? Note down and explore the elements you find important.

*   *   *

People wait in front of embassies hoping to get a visa, asylum status or sometimes even just an interview. Why? Because they think it is worth it. People wait for Wimbledon tickets sleeping in tents on the street in all sorts of weather conditions. Why? Because they think it is worth it.

As Henri Nouwen eloquently said:

«People who wait have received a promise that allows them to wait. They have received something that is at work in them, like a seed that has started to grow. This is very important. We can only really wait if what we are waiting for has already begun for us. So waiting is never a movement from nothing to something. It is always a movement from something to something more.»[50]

I cannot express just how important I find the above quote to be because of the clear way it conceptualises 'waiting'. Read through it again slowly, before moving on.

Which door would you sleep in front of and what are you willing to wait for every day? Draw yourself waiting in front of that door.

How does knowing God will not fail you change your perspective on waiting at His door?

---

[50] *Seeds of Hope*, A Henri Nouwen Reader edited by Robert Durback (Bantam Books, 1989). Quote also found at http://www.athomewithgod.co.uk/Nouwen%20A%20Spirituality%20of%20waiting-1.pdf

Nouwen continues as he highlights the relevance and importance of the current moment in the grander scheme of waiting:

«Active waiting means to be present fully to the moment, in the conviction that something is happening where you are and that you want to be present to it.»

What is happening right now, as you are waiting? What might God be wanting to bring to your attention?

Why not resolve to wait at God's door, however long it takes, till He comes out, knowing fully well that He most certainly will and knowing that when He does, you will be abundantly happy and your life the better for it?

Your prayer:

DAY 11
don't worry

«[...] Hear, O Israel: Today you are on the verge of battle with your enemies. Do not let your heart faint, do not be afraid, and do not tremble nor be terrified because of them; for YHVH your God is He who goes with you, to fight for you against your enemies, to save you.» Deuteronomy 20:3-4

Have you ever picked up one of Roger Hargreaves' books from the children's series Mr Men? There is a certain Mr Worry who worries about everything. If it rains, he worries that his roof will leak, if there is no rain, he worries that all of his plants will die. He also worries about the other Mr Men; one day he meets a wizard who suggests he make a list of all his worries and the wizard will make sure none of them happen. When there is nothing to worry about, Mr Worry is happy for a week, until he becomes worried about not having anything to worry about!

Are you a 'worrier'? Do you know any worriers? Studies have found that worry largely consists of verbal thought, people thinking or talking about what is worrying them. So a pair of scientists decided to test whether engaging in imagery (the RH) rather than verbal processing (the LH) would make a difference. The participants engaged in a silent five-minute period of worry during which one group verbally processed what they were worried about (they were asked to think in words, sentences and questions, as though they were talking to themselves). During that same time the other group explored what was worrying them by using imagery (they were asked to generate an image of the situation, tuning in to what they could see, feel, smell, hear and taste in the image as though they were in it right at that moment). The results revealed that after this 'worry period' the group that used images rather than words to express their worry had less unwanted negative thoughts than the verbal group.[51]

---

[51] It is suggested that one of the main reasons why imagery was more helpful in this context than verbal processing is because imagery is more concrete and helps put things into a more realistic perspective. Verbal thoughts (often 'what if...' - which is LH territory) can easily escalate in one's mind and become catastrophic,

What are you worrying about this very moment? How many items are on your list?

Worry. Fear. Anxiety. Part of the reason we worry is because we are afraid and we are afraid because we do not trust. It seems that God knew that this would be an issue for us human beings since in just this one text, phrases of reassurance are repeated four times.

When broken down, the Hebrew words mean the following:

Don't be discouraged, do not let your inner person lack courage or spirit, do not be afraid, don't expect things in alarm. Do not tremble, shake involuntarily, do not run away, do not let fear overcome you and do not be terrified. Do not dread those who are against you, there is no reason for such intense fear.

Re-read the previous paragraph aloud and insert your name where necessary, telling yourself those very things (insert your name '_____, don't be discouraged...').

God continues to comfort Israel by reassuring them He will go with them and fight their battle for them and He will save them. It will end well for them, to their benefit – there is no reason to worry. The outcome is in their favour. The outcome is in *your* favour.

Like many things, to live this message is easier said than done, but it is simple in its essence: ***do not worry***. If you trust and let Him, God will do the fighting for you; He is on your side and you are not alone. He will deal with whatever you are up against and in the end you will win by His grace. Whatever the outcome, it will be good for you and there is no reason to doubt that, ever, at all.

Take a moment to thoughtfully ponder each of these:

o   God fights my battles for me, on my behalf. I do my part but I am not alone.
o   If I am with God, there is no reason to be afraid. Not one.

---

partly because they are more abstract in nature and not linked to a specific context. Exploring worry topics using imagery also draws on one's autobiographical memory and helps keep the thoughts from becoming more negative and thereby causing more stress. Caroline Stokes and Colette R. Hirsch, "Engaging in imagery versus verbal processing of worry: Impact on negative intrusions in high worriers", *Behaviour, Research and Therapy* 48, vol. 5 (2010), 418-423.

o   God wins, He always wins. I will win because of Him. Whatever happens, whatever the outcome of my battle, it will be good for me.

Ask yourself this question: what am I afraid of? In getting to the answer, imagine an upside-down pyramid (you may want to draw it) – there may be many fears on the top, but as you go along try and narrow them down until you reach the underlying fear from which the others stem. This might not happen today, but if you come back to it you will likely make progress in this process of unearthing the underlying fear. Asking 'why' after you establish a fear will often help you go further down to the root (imagine a child asking an adult 'why' after every answer). Writing out the answers (the 'pyramid') might be helpful as you will not have to struggle to remember them later on if you want to refer back to them.

Once you have gone as far as you feel you can, depict what you have identified as your underlying 'fear' on a piece of paper and give it a name...

*   *   *

Now imagine what your fear could look like if God came, took a pencil, and drew on it, around it, and transformed it into something that is positive.

Draw that adapted and transformed image of your fear. When you have finished, sit in silence for a little while and contemplate your drawing...

*   *   *

How has that fear affected your life until now?

What initially caused it?

What have you worried about in the past?

Now that you are more aware of it, how do you think it might affect you from now on?

Looking back at your fear pyramid, it is easy to see how one initial fear soon breeds a plethora of other fears. Next time you find yourself worrying, fretting and fearing for whatever reason, apply the pyramid, become aware of the root and deal with it at that base level (the sooner the better). The practice will be very worthwhile in the long term and you will begin to feel its liberating effect.

How does it impact your life, daily and practically, knowing that God is in control and that if you continue to stay connected to Him, things will work out well for you?

Your prayer:

DAY 12
guidance

«O YHVH, you have examined me and know me. You know when I sit down or stand up; You discern my thoughts from afar. You measure my travelling and my lying down, and are familiar with all my ways. There is not a word on my tongue that You, O YHVH, do not fully know [...] where can I escape from Your Spirit? Where can I flee from Your presence? [...] If I take the wings of the morning and dwell in the uttermost parts of the sea, even there Your hand will guide me, and Your strength will support me.» Psalms 139:1-4, 7, 9-10

"Clear for take off... Climbing to 5,000 heading to 2020... You're flying straight into the weather, it'll be choppy for the next 100-150 miles... Maintain normal speed... Smooth ride here... Climb to 350... 330 an occasional light chop... You'd have to be above 36,000 to be smooth... We'll go if you approve it... I can't, I'm sorry... OK... Maintain one zero thousand... United 725 contact departure... United 725 contact ground... You are about to leave our zone, your tower is now 269 – have a good night. Thanks, you too."[52]

During long haul flights an airplane will cross great distances that are controlled by several different air traffic control towers. Each time it leaves one zone and enters another there is a formal acknowledgment of that transition between both parties. Wherever the airplane may be there is always a tower that is responsible for taking care of it and it is important that they regularly communicate.

In the text above the Psalmist is acknowledging that God is everywhere and knows everything, much like the communication between the airplane and the control tower. He admits there is not a thought he could have without God being aware of it; there is no place he could go of which God would not know. The Psalmist says even if he were to dwell in the innermost parts of the sea... even there God would guide him and lead

---

[52] An example of snippets of a conversation between the control tower and the airplane pilot; I pieced this together from a United Airlines flight I was on a number of years ago.

him with His right hand. Even there, his 'control tower' would be God and he could trust His guidance.

The depths of the sea are often representative of Chaos in the Bible, the place of darkness and death.[53] On a practical level even today, the depths of the sea are dark and incredibly far away from the surface of 'the rest of the world'. The deepest part is almost 10,000 m (36,000 ft) below sea level and it is said that if Mt. Everest were placed at this location, it would be covered by over one mile of water. It is difficult for us to imagine just how deep that deepest part really is.

But God says even in the darkest, deepest, most remote place you can imagine: if you are there, I am there with you. Remember the kernel, your innermost part? Remember the private dining room? That connection (or its potential) between you cannot be severed no matter what the circumstances may be. No matter where you may find yourself in life, if you want Him to, He is strong enough to reach through to you no matter where you are.

  * *Wherever you are, you are His.*

Yesterday's key thought: no matter what happens, it will be good for you (the outcome is taken care of).

Today's key thought: no matter where you are, God is there with you (the potential for your connection will always be there).

He will always guide you, even if you fall so deep and give up on yourself, thinking you are too messed up, too weak, too average, too unworthy. Even there, *even there*, God will be with you to help you navigate to a better state of mind and being.

Reflect on the airspace communication and imagine what it must be like to be a pilot or an air traffic controller…

Have you ever been a guide to someone? What attributes make someone a good guide? Are there any attributes on your list you would attribute to God? Have you been aware of God's guidance in your life until now? How have you experienced it recently? Note down your observations.

---

[53] Ps. 69:15; 107:23-30; 124:4-5. A wonderful resource for imagery in the Psalms is Othmar Keel, *The Symbolism of the Biblical World: Ancient Near Eastern Iconography and the Book of Psalms*, (Winona Lake: Eisenbrauns, 1997), cf. p. 73-76 for the sea.

Draw your life as a line, roadmap, river or journey. Draw in your lifeline (or even paste in images from magazines/newspapers) things that represent landmarks in your life, internal or external events along the way that are significant to you (especially those which pertain to God's guidance).

*   *   *

Looking at your drawing, what is the first thing you notice? Why?

How many landmarks did you draw?

Are they evenly spread out or did they occur in clusters?

Was God's guidance obvious at the time? Why or why not? If so, when did it become clear?

Are there any patterns concerning your landmarks?

Are there some landmarks that are a little more ambiguous when it comes to God's guidance? Notice what they are and perhaps explore why that may be so.

Would you say your landmarks were more internally discernible or externally observable? Looking at your drawing (without thinking), which landmark is the most emotionally charged, which goes the deepest?

What makes that landmark so significant?

How was God's guidance seen or felt in connection with it?

Take a moment to contemplate the communication between pilot and control tower. How is the communication between you and God in your life? Take another look at your landmarks through this 'filter' of air traffic communication; what do you notice? Were there times you chose to ignore the control tower? Times when the voice seemed almost inaudible? Were there times you were aware of contact even though you were sure you had gone far outside the radar zone?

Write down any additional thoughts, memories or associations that seem important to you...

Your prayer:

balance

«All the ways of a person seem right to him or her, but YHVH probes motives. Entrust your affairs to YHVH, and your plans will succeed.» Proverbs 16:2-3

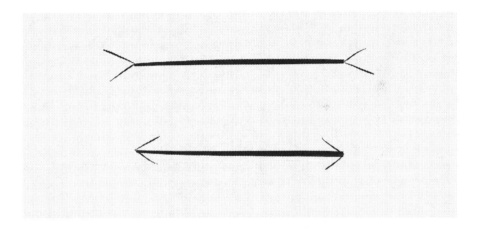

Have a look at the two figures above: of the two vertical lines, which line is longer? What is the illusion? The illusion is that you think the line below is shorter than the one above. And though you might measure the two horizontal lines and prove to yourself that they are identical, nevertheless your eyes will always see one as shorter or longer than the other.

Optical illusions are numerous and varied and the one above (also known as Müller-Lyer's illusion, 1889), demonstrates that two lines of the exact same length are perceived differently depending on which direction the arrows on the end are pointing. Much like the figure above, Edward Titchener's illusion below also reinforces the importance of context and its role in perception.

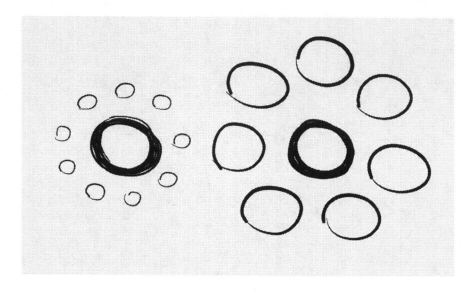

Optical illusions fascinate us because they highlight how our sense of vision can be misguided, how objects and the relationships between them can be misperceived. But illusions are not restricted solely to the world of vision.

«All the ways of a person seem right to him or her...» – the two images seem so completely different from each other yet the inner circle is exactly the same, the vertical lines identical. Of all the options before us, of all the 'figures' we face how are we to know what is true and what is an illusion? If all of our options seem good to us as the text above indicates, then how are we to discern which ones are better than the others? With so much pressure to succeed, the margin for error feels narrow and to know the difference is crucial.

Every day we are under pressure to perform, to be at the top of our game, to always make the best choices and to be able to do everything ourselves. Sometimes we are so self-sufficient, we lose ourselves in a sea of isolation and lonely striving. At face value, many options available to us may be equally good, wise, profitable and salient; yet they are not always what they seem. Often it is only after a few months upon accepting a certain job that its true colours bleed through and we realise, in retrospect, that perhaps it was not the best decision we could have made. But how are we to know?

In today's proverb, two crucial components emerge based on the words 'entrust' (*galal*, גָּלַל) and 'succeed' (*kun*, כּוּן).

Galal literally means to roll, roll up or away or roll together; figuratively, it means to commit and to trust.

Kun literally means to erect, stand perpendicular, to set up; figuratively it means to establish something, to fix and prepare it, make prosperous, stable and ready, balance out. Both *galal* and *kun* are layered with meaning but for now we will focus on these aspects.

In other words, the key components can be summarised as:

o   what we do (roll up) and
o   what God does (balances out)

An in-depth analysis of the individual Hebrew words in this passage reveals the deeper meaning. The essence of the proverb is this:

The way I live my life, as an individual, may seem acceptable by my personal standards. But God, the Eternal One, He measures, arranges and balances out my life, my anger, my fears, all my expressions and functions. God says to me, roll your things up (actions good or bad, the things I am and have) and roll it in My direction; I, the Eternal One, will prepare and fix, provide for, make stable and proper all your intentions and plans (whether good or bad), the things you imagine, what you intend to do and what you think about.

Have you ever been afraid of making the wrong decision? Fear of failure is crippling. God is systematically addressing your fears and trying to free you from them, one by one. He is plainly telling you that if you completely trust Him and let Him have His way, He will always balance you out, make your way proper and stable. He will make you entirely ready and prepared for the next step on your path.

Remember Day 1, the little man in the eye and our reflection? Consider this: when we are close to God we can see ourselves in His eyes; in other words, who we are is clear, our purpose in life and our worth as human beings. Much like looking at an image at close range, we can see the pixels to the minutest detail. But if we move away from Him we begin to lose sight of our reflection in His eyes and what was once obvious and stable is now prone to becoming fragmented and distorted. The image now begins to blur and fade and we may not even be sure what the image is or if there is an image at all. Doubt and a lack of confidence follow as we begin to search for another 'mirror', another source of reflection that will show us who we are. The greater the distance between God and ourselves, the greater the distortion of our view of life, of God, and ourselves. The closer we are, the clearer and more truthful our perceptions.

Take a walk outside in your area and keep an eye out for small stones, leaves, bark, anything you are drawn to (and could write on). When you have done this, consider the options before you: the choices you need to make, the fears you cling to, things you worry about, things you wish you could just hand over to someone and know for certain they would turn out all right... Write them out one by one on these objects you have found. Roll them all up together in a cloth or paper or whatever you choose, tie it up and put it in a safe place. This will be a reminder of your surrender to God and His promise to balance it all out. When you have done this, write a letter to God in which you are telling Him what you are rolling up and giving to Him to take care of for you.

*   *   *

Your part:
Rolling up sticks, twigs, stones, paper, tying them up and keeping them.

Writing a letter to God telling Him what you are rolling up, what you are giving over to His control for Him to take care of for you.

God's part:
Balancing things out, taking care of you.

«Here I sit with warp strings stretched out before me. With a hedge system I change positions of alternate warps to create the shed. I insert my threads, weave a row, use hedges to alternate the warps to form a second shed. I insert other threads, weave a second row, once again change the warp in preparation for another row. In this way I am constantly working with a dyad fundamental to my art. One, two. Front, back. Odd, even. Vertical, horizontal. Left to right, right to left. Opposites, coordinates, always present before me. I weave into relationship the odds and evens of things.»[54]

Like a master weaver, God weaves into relationship the odds and ends of our life to continuously produce a stunning tapestry.

After some time (days, weeks or months), go back to your bundle, untie it and notice how things have developed with what you left in His keeping. When you notice that something you have placed in there is no longer an issue, write it in your journal, taking note of how God took care of that in particular; then discard that stone, leaf, etc. You might want to replace it and keep your collection updated. In general, this will help you monitor the progress in certain areas of your life and allow you to be aware of how God is taking care of those things for you.

*   *   *

With God, you are always on track.
God makes your way, your life, clean.
Completely trust Him.
He will balance everything out.

Your prayer:

---

[54] David Jongeward, *Weaver of Worlds*, (Rochester: Vermont, 1990), 143-144.

DAY 14

promise

«YHVH will work out His plans for my life – for Your faithful love (chesed), YHVH, endures forever. Don't let me go, for You made me.» Psalms 138:8

Brand.
What comes to mind?
Coca Cola, Apple, Amazon?
According to marketing experts, a brand is a one-of-a-kind promise about who you are, what you stand for and what unique and meaningful benefits you deliver. A brand is strong when it consistently lives up to its promise every single time you and I come into contact with its name, message and business. As it goes, great brands are not only known, they are loved.

In 1969 American philosopher John R. Searle defined a promise as a *commitment on the part of a speaker to accomplish a future action*. He stated that the fulfilment of a promise hinges on two conditions: a *preparatory condition* (the listener wants the promised action to be accomplished) and a *sincerity condition* (the speaker intends to accomplish the action).[55]

Psychologists Josie Bernicot & Virginie Laval[56] used that premise to determine how children understand promises and process them. The children were given a story completion task in the form of successive frames that each reveal an aspect of the story. The experimenter told the beginning of the story whose main character was a young boy named Bill, and each frame of the story had a 'speaker' and a 'listener'. The story was told in three of four frames in a story board manner.

FRAME 1 – Theme - either the listener wanted the speaker to keep his/her promise, or the listener did not want the speaker to keep his/her promise

---

[55] John R. Searle, *Speech acts*, (Cambridge: Cambridge University Press, 1969).
[56] J. Bernicot and V. Laval, "Promises in French children: comprehension and metapragmatic knowledge", *Journal of Pragmatics* 35 (1996), 101-122.

FRAME 2 – Promise – Bill makes a promise to his friend/parents that was phrased in one of the following ways (e.g. *promise-to-act*: I promise I'll wash my bike; *future-action*: I'll wash my bike; *predictive-assertion*: my bike will be washed).

FRAME 3 – Promise fulfillment – the picture shows Bill completing the action that corresponded to the action in Frame 2

FRAME 4 – End of story - the child was to complete the story by choosing one of two pictures proposed for this frame: 1) shows the listener with a clearly discontented facial expression and the words 'unhappy', or 2) shows the listener with a clearly happy facial expression and the words 'happy'.

When the child chose one of the two options, the experimenter then asked the child to explain why he/she had made that choice. The results showed that, among other things, children as young as age three and six are able to take into account cues that reveal the listener's desires (whether a person wants the promise to be fulfilled) and the speaker's intentions (whether a person intends to fulfil it). They learn to detect the likelihood of the promise being fulfilled (the speaker's intentions) first, and later on learn to recognise whether a person would like the promise to be fulfilled (the listener's desires). Interestingly, though children begin to understand the intricacies of promises at an early age, it is only at the age of ten onwards that they begin to make remarks concerning the speaker's intentions (discussing and analysing whether that person really intends to fulfil his/her promise). We learn of promises and their meaning from a very young age and most often this sets the tone for our attitude towards them for many years to come.

Even as adults, when a promise is made we expect it to be fulfilled. We expect people to be true to their word. This is not always the case and we are often disappointed yet we still hope, expect and long for fulfilment. This is true for big things (personal relationships, business transactions) as well as smaller things, such as expecting a laundry detergent to remove the stains in my shirt if that is its promise to me.

When it comes to the things in your life, God is continually seeing them through, completing them, evening them out and 'perfecting' them. «For Your faithful love, O Lord, endures *forever*.» He is the brand that never fails, always living up to His promises. The word 'forever' here (*olam*, עוֹלָם) is 'a designation of time extending so far that it is lost to our sight and comprehension in darkness and invisibility [...] [*Olam*] is not an endlessly long time but simply a *boundless time*.'[57] (emphasis added). Simply said, we cannot fully grasp just how faithful He truly is.

When you keep allowing God to lead you and have completely given Him freedom concerning the outcome(s), He *promises* to complete what He has planned for you, and since He is faithful you know you can rely on what He says. When He says He will come through for you, He will. If He says He will remove the stains from your life, He will. If He says He will resolve a particular problem, help you with something, you can be absolutely certain that He will. When, it does not matter. *He will.*

Take a moment now to quietly bring to memory the most meaningful promises in your life, noticing those that first come to mind... They can be promises you have made to others, to yourself, or those others have made to you. Regardless whether you kept your promise or whether they kept their promise, which were the most meaningful and which impacted you the most? Once you have identified those key promises, draw each promise.

*   *   *   **

Take a look at the promises you have drawn...

How many of them are your promises to others?

How many of them are promises others made to you?

---

[57] Thorleif Boman, *Hebrew Thought Compared with Greek*, (New York, NY: Norton & Company, 1970), 151. This is the first time I have quoted Boman in this book but there will be a few more references throughout the remainder of the book so for those readers who are in the field of biblical studies I need to say the following. I am aware of the debates surrounding the concept of 'Hebrew thought' and the criticisms that James Barr directed at Boman's line of thought (based on Whorf, based on Humboldt). However I aim not to throw out the baby with the bath water, recognising that Boman made some very interesting and valid points. My own linguistic research of the figurative use of body part terminology in the Old Testament in certain aspects echoes some of Boman's views and arguments. For a more updated examination of language and its influence on thought I recommend: Dedre Genter and Susan Goldwin-Meadow, *Language in Mind: Advances in the Study of Language and Thought*, (Cambridge, MA: Bradford Books, 2003) and Guy Deutscher, *Through the Language Glass: Why the World Looks Different in Other Languages*, (London: Arrow, 2011).

Are they equal in number?

Reflect on what makes each of them significant for you.

How many of them, yours or theirs, were fulfilled promises, promises kept?

How many, if any, were broken promises, either 'permanently' or temporarily?

Imagine that all of the promises you have drawn are emotionally charged, ranging from 1 (low) – 10 (high). Without giving yourself a moment to think, take a look at all the promises you have drawn and rank them accordingly.

Notice the one that ranked the highest...

Why that one in particular?

Did you expect that or are you somewhat surprised?

What is it about that promise that has made it more powerful in its effect on you than the others?

Now for a moment, contemplate some of the things you have begun in your life and have not completed (perhaps note them down). What were the biggest obstacles in preventing you from completing them? At the same time, consider some of the things you did complete in the past. What were the key reasons you completed them as opposed to the others you did not? How might all of these factors affect your attitude towards promises, yours and those of others?

*   *   *

Violet Ho and her colleagues discovered that personality (specifically, the trait of Agreeableness)[58] affects not only how a person *reacts* to a broken promise, but how that person will judge the *seriousness* of the breach.[59] The situation also needs to be taken into consideration, however overall when

---

[58] The personality trait of Agreeableness (one of the Big Five as defined by Costa & McCrae, 1987) is an individual's preference for interacting with others and consists of six facets: straightforwardness, trust in others, altruism, compliance to others, modesty, and tendermindedness (i.e. sympathy and concern for others). A person high in this trait will tend to experience negative emotions less intensely, be able to manage their emotions well, be less likely to negatively label the person that broke the promise and generally be trusting of others.

[59] Violet T. Ho, L. R. Weingart and D. M. Rousseau, "Responses to broken promises: Does personality matter?" *Journal of Vocational Behavior*, 65 (2004), 276-293.

there is a severe breach of promise, regardless of personality traits most people will tend to react in the same way. Essentially, if an individual feels that a major and consequential loss will result from a broken promise, he or she will naturally react more negatively to it than to a minor breach in which an unimportant loss occurs.

Whatever our personality type and traits, we all fear the loss that can occur were promises to be broken. This fear is likely to affect how we feel about God and trusting His promises.

Consider this, today God is saying to you: *I promise to fulfil My plans for your life.*

What does this mean to you? How might this affect your daily life and plans?

Note down your findings, observations and relevant thoughts, memories or associations…

Your prayer:

DAY 15
pliability

«Delight yourself in YHVH, and He will give you your heart's desires. Commit your journey to YHVH. Trust Him, and He will bring it to pass.» Psalms 37:4-5

Did you stretch this morning before you got of bed? How about when you exercise, do you stretch each time? Stretching in the morning is a natural way of loosening up your muscles in a relaxing way that aids blood circulation. In case you have not already come across the name, Novak Đoković is a Serbian tennis player who has consistently been at the top of world tennis for quite a number of years. While watching Wimbledon I have heard John McEnroe comment on Đoković's flexibility countless times during his matches, and photographs of him in action reveal his unusual elasticity.[60] How exactly does flexibility matter? To be flexible means to have a good range of motion in our joints, and in Đoković's case that flexibility enables him to reach for the ball as he slides on the surface of the court, legs wide apart, without tearing a muscle and seriously injuring himself.

In every movement we make there are two groups of muscles at work – protagonistic muscles (those in favour of the movement, causing it to happen) and antagonistic muscles (those opposing the movement and determining the amount of flexibility). In order to have a healthy, moving body, we need both types of muscles to function as best as they can. While physical flexibility is important for our overall health, flexibility is not just a term confined to tennis or physical activities.

Flexibility seems to be one of the buzzwords for organisations, systems, approaches, labour markets, and the list goes on. Even when speaking of people, if you and I are flexible that means we have a range of different appropriate behavioural responses that we can choose from in the situations

---

[60] 'Đoković has incredibly good flexibility because of his core area; he has got this incredible variety of serve.' Neil Harman, Tennis Correspondent quoting John McEnroe in his article in The Times on June 17, 2008 http://thetim.es/dGb9Sp

we face. Just like Đoković, the more flexible and pliable we are the lesser our discomfort and the greater our capabilities.

What does flexiblity have to do with the passage above? In this text the Hebrew word 'delight' means 'to be soft, pliable, have delight'. It speaks of adaptability in the sense that we are pliable in God's hands; just like a good coach, God stretches us and shapes us as He sees fit for our own benefit. The more pliable we are, the easier His job and the less painful those movements will be for us.

When we are pliable, open-minded and trusting, we can allow God to stretch and shape us and progress as a result. Much like our muscles, there are protagonists and antagonists, contending forces that create tension when a part of us wants to grow and a part of us wants to preserve the *status quo*. If we tense up then the process of transformation will be impeded and even more painful. Maintaining a pliable attitude allows God to give us what we desire in a way that will always be the best possible option (and often one we have not even considered!).

What underlies our pliability is trust. If we know our coach or mentor is an expert in that field, if he has a proven track record of successes and good training techniques, then we are more likely to want him as our coach. We are also more willing to trust his judgment. In the same way if we trust God and give Him our whole life, every last bit of it, in return He fulfils what we ask for in a complete way. How is this related to delight? Delight and pliability are closely linked.

* We can only be pliable when we trust the hands that hold us.

The essence of the text might be captured as follows.

Allow yourself to be moulded by God and enjoy it, be happy that it is that way. If you do, He will give you, deliver, restore without fail what you ask of Him regarding your feelings, will and intellect. Roll up your life, entirely, as you now live it and give it to Him. Trust in Him, go to Him for refuge, be sure of what He says and He will do it, thoroughly, to the end, accomplishing His purpose in your life.

Howard E. Gardner introduced a broader understanding of 'intelligence' to the world, claiming there were several types of intelligence, not just one.[61] Gardner saw mental and physical activity as related and one of those types of intelligence was *bodily-kinesthetic intelligence*. This refers to a body-centred intelligence that informs how one knows and experiences the world. It stands in contrast to the Cartesian view in which knowledge is primarily in the mind. Philosopher and psychologist John Dewey viewed bodily experience as the primal basis for meaning, thinking, knowing and communication,[62] however it was philosopher Maurice Merleau-Ponty who laid the foundation for a contemporary, Western, non-dualist ontology[63] of the body; his main tenet was that we live in the world through 'a union between the psychic and the physiological.'[64]

Your creative exercise today involves physically stretching, very, very slowly... Find a quiet place (no music) where you will be undisturbed, preferably outside in the fresh air... Go through a range of stretching exercises at a *very slow* pace, bearing in mind that stretching the muscle is only part of the exercise. The aim is to stretch slowly, giving yourself time to be mentally present, to be aware of your body as you stretch,

---

[61] Gardner's types of intelligence: linguistic, logical-mathematical, musical, spatial, bodily-kinesthetic, interpersonal and intrapersonal. Howard E. Gardner, *Multiple Intelligences: The theory in practice*, (New York: Basic Books, 1993).

[62] Mitchell S. Kossak, "Therapeutic attunement: A transpersonal view of expressive arts therapy", *The Arts in Psychotherapy*, 36 (2009), 13-18.

[63] Ontology deals with the nature of being, part of the branch of philosophy that deals with abstract concepts (e.g. being, knowing, time, space, etc.).

[64] Maurice Merleau-Ponty, *Phenomenology of perception* (London: Routledge & Keegan Paul, 1962), 80. Early Greek philosophers varied in their understanding of what the human being is, however after Plato the idea of a dualist human being (separate body and soul) was prominent on the philosophical scene. This dualism did not originate with Plato nor with Greek philosophers in general (although a particular strand certainly did), however the Western tradition today is a descendant of that philosophical heritage which means that this conceptualisation of the human being has been taken on board. What is important to note is that not only was it thought that the human being consists of a body and soul, but the body was deemed base and horrible, a prison and a tomb for the perfect, immortal soul. Over time the soul was elevated as the pure essence of the human, while the body was something that was to be tolerated until the final liberation after death. This understanding of the human being stands in stark contrast to the biblical understanding that is much more in line with Merleau-Ponty's. In fact it is only against the backdrop of this continued, prominent dualism that the contributions of those such as Merleau-Ponty gain particular significance.

your muscles, the tension, the barrier between discomfort and pain (be careful not to cross the barrier into pain)... As you stretch, be aware of your breathing... Focus your attention away from your LH self-talk... Our bodies and our inner being are intertwined so in the quietness, as you go through these exercises, notice what surfaces regarding your inner flexibility and pliability in God's hands...[65]

*   *   *

How did it feel to stretch?

What thoughts or impressions came to mind as you were stretching?

Reflect on the exercises you did, stretching the various muscles and muscle groups...

Which muscle was a little tighter and felt more uncomfortable to stretch?

Do you use that muscle frequently? What might be causing that discomfort?

Which muscle or group of muscles would you compare yourself to? Why?

How pliable are you in God's hands?

Would you say you are more or less pliable than you were five years ago, one year ago, six months ago?

Practically speaking, what can you do to become even more pliable in God's hands?

How do we know how flexible we are, physically speaking? It is only when we stretch that we realise our limits and capabilities. How do we know how flexible we are, spiritually speaking? It is only when we face situations that 'stretch' us that we become aware of just how far we are willing to go and also how much training we still need.

«Gesture is embodied thought.» - Malcolm MacLachlan

Next time you are tempted to think of your body as just physical, remember today and the link between inner and outer. Next time you

---

[65] Something along these lines might help to give some examples of possible exercises: http://www.sportsscience.co/flexibility/whole-body-stretching-routine/

catch yourself thinking of the physical and mental as separate, think of Gardner and Merleau-Ponty.

If possible, do these stretching exercises every day and notice your progress in just a week, fortnight or a month. Perhaps you can find ways to do the same with your inner pliability...

Your prayer:

DAY 16
light

«For You light my lamp; YHVH my God enlightens my darkness.»
Psalms 18:28

Do you have the lights on at the moment? Have you ever been without electricity? Electricity is part of nature and aside from being one of our most widely used forms of energy, it is something most of us cannot imagine our 21st century lives without. Electricity is actually what is known as an energy carrier, meaning that we get electricity from the conversion of other sources of energy such as coal, natural gas, nuclear and renewable sources such as wind power and solar energy.

In the late 1800s it was Nikola Tesla who pioneered the generation, transmission and use of alternating current electricity, which reduced the cost of transmitting electricity over long distances. Tesla's inventions used electricity to bring lighting into our homes and to power industrial machines (and nowadays even our cars!). Not surprisingly, Tesla was exceptionally skilful in using both his hemispheres to generate extraordinary ideas and their practical solutions.[66]

Though Tesla was exceptional in harnessing this natural resource, it is clear that neither he, you, nor I could produce electricity. I can install a light bulb in my room, plant myself on a chair and stare at it, waiting for it to light up, but unless there is electricity the bulb is utterly useless and

---

[66] Nikola Tesla reported using visual mental imagery when working on his inventions. He used a visual image to conceive the details of the machine he was working on, and noted that his 'mental pictures' were more vivid than any blueprint. He would also run mental 'dry runs' to examine the machine for any wear and tear over weeks of time. Like Tesla, Albert Einstein also reported visualising himself travelling at the speed of light alongside a beam of light, and observing the appearance of the beam. This 'thought experiment' helped him to see that light is not an electromagnetic field with no velocity, and to realise that such a thing did not exist. S. M. Kosslyn, *Ghosts in the Mind's Machine: Creating and Using Images in the Brain* (New York, NY: W. W. Norton, 1983).

I will sooner grow old and wrinkled staring at that bulb than will light suddenly appear. In today's passage the Psalmist says God lights his lamp, that God enlightens his darkness.

It seems that David was onto something when he wrote what he did – he recognised that there had to be a source elsewhere, outside of himself, that would bring about the light. David has (or is) the lamp, but he is unable to enlighten his own darkness; God does for him that which electricity does for a light bulb.

Imagine you are a light bulb… Draw what you see in your imagination…

*   *   *

Once you have finished your drawing, imagine you are interviewing the light bulb and electricity. Write down the interview as though it were a transcript of a live interview and let it flow, without thinking about what you are writing.

Questions posed to the light bulb can be about its history, functions, likes and dislikes, its daily routine, its hopes for the future… Here are a few to get you started but also notice any questions that surface that may not be in the list below.

What kind of a bulb are you?

Where are you?

How do you feel in your setting?

How did you come to be where you are?

Is there a steady supply of electricity where you are?

If so (or if not), how does that affect you?

Are you alone or are there other bulbs with or near you? Why or why not?

How often are you shining?

Do you randomly flicker on and off?

How do you feel when you are plugged in?

And when you are not?

How do you get plugged in to begin with?

What 'switches you off'?

Questions posed to electricity (its source) can be along the lines of:

What do you do?

What is your main purpose?

How exactly do you light up a light bulb?

What brings you joy?

Where do you come from?

Where do you spend most of your time?

How many light bulbs do you supply with energy?

Let your imagination wander as you pose your questions and enjoy the interview!

*   *   *

In quiet contemplation, notice what you have written down. What have you learnt from the interview? Did it go as you expected, were there any surprises? Whom were you more inspired to interview? Which of your two interviewees was more talkative? What observations can you make about this transcript?

If, based on today's passage, God is electricity and we are light bulbs, how is the dynamic between these two elements expressed in your interview? What insight can you draw from it?

How is your connection to God? Have you experienced Him as the source of light in your life? Do you rely on Him as such? Being a light bulb is already a wonder in itself, but in order to be connected, you have to flip the switch otherwise the electric current will not reach you.

Is being a light bulb enough? Is eating, sleeping, working to pay a mortgage, dining with friends and eventually dying enough? What is the point of being a light bulb if it never gets connected?

Why not dare to live more fully, to try and get (and stay) connected to God and see if it will bring more light into your life? An extraordinary light bulb is one that is connected and shining, enlightening others as it fulfils its purpose. At the end of the day, is that not what light bulbs are for?

Your prayer:

DAY 17

meaning

«Blessed be YHVH, for He has heard the voice of my earnest prayer. YHVH is my strength and my shield; my heart trusts in Him and He helps me. My heart greatly rejoices and with my song I praise Him.» Psalms 28:6-7

When speaking of biblical narration as understood by the Hebrew writers, Hebrew scholar and professor Robert Alter says:

«Meaning [...] was conceived as a *process*, requiring continual revision – both in the ordinary sense and in the etymological sense of seeing again – continual suspension of judgment, weighing of multiple possibilities, brooding over the gaps in the information provided.»[67] (emphasis added)

When we experience something, we assign it a meaning that is relevant and significant for us at that moment in time. However if we revisit that event in our mind after some time has passed, we often find that either the significance has faded or the experience has taken on a new meaning, as though more dimensions were added to the same image.

This is what happened regarding my climb up Mt. Sinai – it meant one thing to me at the time, yet when I thought about it again at a later stage, its shape and form grew more complex, becoming deeper and wider and with multiple layers. It is in this sense that meaning was considered a process; meaning is fluid in its nature and we cannot initially grasp all the inherent complexities, so we benefit from repeated contemplation, from assessment and a fresh perspective after the passing of some time.

Today's passage is a moment of recognition and acknowledgment of God who offers His strength and God who provides protection, God who is trustworthy and who helps the struggling human being. It is yet another confirmation that He hears, responds and cares. He is not passive, but rather actively engaged and invested in His relationship with you.

---

[67] Robert Alter, *The Art of Biblical Narrative*, (New York: Basic Books, 1983), 12.

Life seems to be increasingly fast paced as time goes by. So many things compete for our attention and we often reach the end of our day exhausted, not having accomplished everything we had intended. Amidst all the hubbub and frenzy of our daily lives it seems to me that we need time to listen, to contemplate and be in a place of quiet, within and without. This quiet time has proven to be fruitful and necessary for me if I am to live more fully.

Approach today as a time of assessment, bearing in mind that meaning is essentially a process. Today is a time to revisit the ground you have covered and consider what you have experienced so far in this process. Reflect on your progress, take stock, cast a glance backward at what has transpired and see if you can connect a few dots...

What have you learnt?

How have you felt?

What have you thought about?

Which Days have spoken to you more clearly than others?

Is there something you notice now about the days that have passed that you did not notice at the time?

Is there something that still remains a mystery that you wonder about?

Is there a particular reoccurring theme?

Looking at your artwork from the passed days, what do you notice?

Do any patterns emerge?

Does anything catch your eye?

Note down these and any other observations that surface...

*　　*　　*

«Life must be lived forward, but can only be understood backwards.» - Søren Kierkegaard

Consider what you are thankful for in light of what you have written above. Perhaps you can begin to make a habit of pausing to reflect and acknowledging where you are, where you have been and where you are headed...

Your prayer:

DAY 18
safe haven

«Trust in Him at all times, O people; pour out your heart before Him; God is a refuge for us.» Psalms 62:8

Do you feel safe right now? Yes or no?

Refuge – now that is not really a word we hear often these days. Refugees, on the other hand, that one we seem to hear quite frequently, especially as I write this. Maybe we have heard the word 'refugees' one time too many and have become too desensitised to stop and think about what it really means and how it is connected to 'refuge'. A refugee is 'a person who has been forced to heave their country in order to escape war, persecution, or natural disaster.'[68]

UNHCR statistics from 2013 reveal that 51.2 million people were forcibly displaced worldwide, some forced to try to find refuge on foreign soil, others displaced within their own countries searching for solace and a place to call home. The UNHCR states that an average of 32,200 individuals per day were forced to leave their homes and find protection elsewhere.[69] In June 2015, UNHCR estimated that almost 1,153,300 refugees needed resettlement globally .[70] As I am writing this the situation has only worsened.

To make matters worse, though one may be on the run from one's home or home country, sometimes one does not necessarily 'qualify' as a refugee. Whilst working in Yemen I met a young Somali man who had left his wife and children back in his home country (also known as the source country) while he came to Yemen (known as the host country) to try and find a way to help them join him there. Unfortunately he did not

---

[68] https://en.oxforddictionaries.com/definition/refugee
[69] UNHCR Global Trends Document 2013, http://www.unhcr.org/5399a14f9.html
[70] https://www.amnesty.org/en/latest/news/2015/10/global-refugee-crisis-by-the-numbers/

automatically acquire refugee status,[71] which practically meant that the authorities were hunting him down in order to deport him back to his home country. Were he to return to Somalia he would surely be killed, yet he could not stay in this 'host' country because he was there without an official status of any kind. Far from finding a refuge, this young man was a 'nobody', all alone, belonging nowhere and completely rejected.

In Hebrew there are two words that mean 'to trust'. One you learnt on DAY 9, *'to hide for refuge'* (*batach*, בָּטַח) and it is this word that is used in today's passage. The other word means *'to flee for protection'* (*chasah*, חָסָה) and is found in other passages (such as Psalms 61:4) and is conceptually connected to our topic today.

On DAY 8 we mentioned how often words such as 'love' and 'hope' can seem abstract and this can also apply to the concept of trust. Today's passage will continue to build on what you learnt about trust on DAY 9 and what follows should help make 'trust' even more vivid.

In order to understand the concept of trust more fully as found in the biblical text, we need to know the background that would have been familiar to the author of today's passage. This background knowledge most likely shaped his understanding of trust, especially in relation to God.

In the book of Joshua (chapter 20), as ancient Israel was being established as a nation with its own territory, God tells the Israelites to choose six cities that will be places of refuge for those who unintentionally take the life of another. What would usually happen is – as is also not uncommon in some cultures today – a member of the family who had lost a loved one would be enraged and seek revenge. As a result, one loss of life would easily be followed by another, and that one by another, and so it is evident how things could rapidly spiral out of control. To prevent people from taking such matters into their own hands (especially in such a state of mind), six cities were chosen as safe havens for those who had accidentally taken the life of another. If the offender managed to get to one of the safe cities before getting caught, he was let in and protected. The offender stayed in the safe city until either their case was tried, or until the

---

[71] Not all refugees acquire automatic refugee status upon entering a host country. Depending on the host country and the source country of the individual (and other factors), refugees must be interviewed by government officials in order to determine their status as a refugee (details are found in the UNHCR Handbook on Procedure and Criteria in determining refugee status).

High Priest in that city died, in which case the offender was free to go back home from which they had fled. There were three cities on each side of the River Jordan which meant that everyone, Israelites and foreigners alike, had equal opportunity to reach one of them should they have so needed.

Now remember what the words 'to trust' mean in Hebrew: *to hide for refuge, to flee for protection.*

When the Psalmist wrote about trust it is most likely that he had in mind this concept of safe cities as it would have been well known in his culture. This imagery is embedded in the 'trust' we encounter in the passage above: "Trust... God is a refuge..."

Imagine a person who is hunted down, desperate to get to one of these cities in time, knowing that when they do, they will be accepted, they will be safe. When we trust others we make them our temporary refuge, allowing them to hold and hopefully guard what we have shared of ourselves with them. But human refuges are not impenetrable and often the place of refuge becomes a place of great exposure and vulnerability. The difference is that God's invitation is: 'Trust me, come to Me, I am that refuge for you, I will protect you, I will keep you safe from everyone and everything, just come, you know where I am.'

Jesus is my city of refuge, my safe place, to Him I can flee, in Him I can take refuge. I make mistakes, many, even really serious ones, and then I run to Him. He lets me in, He gives me a place to live, to settle down. When others hunt me down like prey wanting to harm me, He doesn't let them – He keeps them away, protects me. I have full immunity in Him, because of Him.

* *Where you fall short, God provides a way.*

The closest concept we have to safe cities today is that of *safe houses* that protect battered spouses, witnesses of crimes, victims of sexual assault, abused children... These houses are for those who are in dire need of safety, whose very lives depend on it.

Take a few moments now and, allowing your mind to freely wander, imagine a safe space, a place of refuge... Depict what you see in a drawing...

*   *   *

Holding your drawing in your hands, have a look at the place of refuge... what do you see?

If you were to describe this place, what are the first three words that spring to mind?

Elaborate these three words in your mind, as though you were telling a friend what those three words mean to you...

Take note of what those three words are describing... (for example, are they referring to the exterior, interior, location or perhaps how the person inside it feels?)

Do these words bring up any other associations for you?

Notice of what material your safe place is made. Of what do places like that remind you? How would you describe the environment of the safe place?

Note down your observations and if you feel you are drawn to explore certain aspects of this exercise, perhaps if one question seems to have 'struck a nerve' more than another, follow it and make note of your reflections...

*   *   *

At the beginning when I asked you if you felt safe I guess you would immediately, perhaps without even noticing, have thought of your physical safety. But as we are reminded today, safety is more than just being in a place where our physical body is not being actively harmed. We need mental, emotional and spiritual safety, a place of respite from what is often a raging storm. Consider how your drawing of your safe place ties in with today's text and in what ways you find refuge in God...

Your prayer:

DAY 19
Listen

«Why do you spend money for what is not bread, and work for that which does not satisfy? Listen to Me, and eat what is good, and let your soul delight in abundance.» Isaiah 55:2

Have you ever considered that hearing and listening involve much more than merely using one's ears? Dame Evelyn Glennie, the only full-time professional classical percussion soloist to date, is renowned for her ability to 'hear' sound with her whole body. At a young age she became profoundly deaf and whilst many dissuaded her from seriously pursuing her love of music, her piano teacher helped her, teaching her to recognise notes on the piano by refining her ability to detect vibration. In doing so he played a crucial role in the path she was to follow.

Today she performs barefoot in order to experience the sound more fully, and she can distinguish the rough pitch of notes by associating where on her body she feels the sound. In her exploration of sound, aside from playing on a large variety of conventional percussion instruments (such as the congas, cymbals, maracas, taiko drums, timpani etc.), she uses anything from flowerpots, pieces of scaffolding to kitchen utensils and other ordinary objects.[72]

From infancy, sound is important in our finding a place in the world. It all begins in the womb when we hear the voice of our mother and identify her as a sound. Yet even then, we are listening with our whole body; our whole being is hearing and feeling the sound, the vibration and movement of the voice.

If we take the 'listening' aspect from the realm of music and transfer it to that of communication, we discover that listening means much more than detecting the sound patterns we perceive as words as we interact with

---

[72] To know more about Dame Evelyn Glennie and her love of music and sound, I recommend the documentary entitled "Touch the Sound". More information is available on her website www.evelyn.co.uk

another person. We detect the tone of their voice and notice how and if the tone matches their words. We also 'listen' to our interlocuters when we notice the way their hands are crossed, how their eyes fall to the floor when they talk about sensitive subjects, how they fiddle about when they want to avoid something. We unconsciously analyse this as they speak and unconsciously respond accordingly.

In essence we all 'listen' and 'hear' with our whole body but most of the time the majority of us are not aware of it. God says: 'Listen to Me, and eat what is good, and let your soul delight in abundance.'

«Music is the most spiritual of arts.» - H. Scherchen

«The first prerequisite for listening to music is so obvious that it almost seems ludicrous to mention, yet it is often the single element that is absent: to pay attention and to give the music your concentrated effort as an active listener.» - William Schuman

In today's creative task you will be what Schuman refers to as an 'active listener' (you will listen to the three pieces of music listed below).[73] As you listen to each piece be aware of your body, how the sound resonates, where and how it feels, how your body is interacting with the sound. Notice how the music moves you, what emotions surface, what images appear in your mind, memories or impressions...

As Schuman writes in the Introduction to Aaron Copland's book *What to Listen for in Music*, sounds in music are organised and they have intellectual as well as emotional appeal.[74] When the piece of music begins, recognise the melody that is presented early on and it will help guide you as you follow it along through the musical narrative. Notice the rhythm (e.g. what is it like, does it change, is it dominant or in the background?) and the range of intensity throughout the piece.

As you listen to each composition, approach it like a painting: look at it from afar, taking it in as a whole. Then move in a little closer and look at one section of it at a time, here a little, there a little, listen to one

---

[73] If you do not have these pieces in your personal music collection, they can be found online, on YouTube.

[74] Aaron Copland, *What to Listen for in Music*, (New York: New American Library, 2002).

instrument, then another... notice any patterns that may arise as you listen... Listening to one composition a few times will help you observe the nuances that often go unnoticed yet make the whole so meaningful.

When you feel you have spent enough time listening, write down your impressions and how they relate to your listening to God...

Ideally you will listen to pieces of music you will not already have strong associations with (much like a blank canvas to paint on), so in case you do in fact know the compositions below very well, I would suggest listening to a similar piece from the same composer.

1. Nuages (Debussy)
2. Blue as the Turquoise Night of Neyshabur – Yo Yo Ma Silk Road Ensemble[75]
3. Prelude in C sharp minor (Rachmaninov)[76]

*   *   *

«Sounds carry *intelligence*. Ideas, feelings and memories are triggered by sounds. If you are too narrow in your awareness of sounds, you are likely to be disconnected from your environment. More often than not, urban living causes narrow focus and disconnection [...] *compassion (spiritual development)* and *understanding* comes from listening [...] in this way, discovery and exploration can take place. New fields of thought can be opened and the individual may be expanded and find opportunity

---

[75] Silk Road Journeys: When Strangers Meet – "For the uninitiated Western listener, the music requires some getting used to. Much of it is based on rhythmic ostinatos. The melodies use Oriental scales; the intonation is untempered; the music seems all color, texture, and atmosphere, without what might be called themes; and repetition takes the place of development. Contrast is achieved through sudden change, buildup by adding instruments." (product description on Amazon). Bear this in mind as you listen. https://www.youtube.com/watch?v=2byHdBqyfbM

[76] The reason why instrumental (non-vocal) pieces have been selected is because melodies are generally more dominant in eliciting emotions as opposed to lyrics. S. O. Ali and Z. F. Peynircioglu Z. F., "Songs and emotions: are lyrics and melodies equal partners?", *Psychology of Music*, 34 (2006), 511-534. Also lyrics can be distracting, as they do not allow the necessary space needed as do instrumental pieces. Again, if you do not have the three pieces above in your own collection, you can find them on YouTube.

to connect in new ways to communities of interest. Practice enhances openness.»[77] (emphasis added)

What did you notice as you listened to the compositions?

What were your impressions, what nuances did you detect?

What images came to mind?

Was there a common thread in your experience of all three pieces?

How were they different one from the other?

If you had to describe each piece to a friend without them ever hearing it, what would you say or do to help them experience it?

Now consider listening in relation to God...

What do you notice when you listen to what God is saying to you?

Do you get a general sense of the message, or do you notice details, one at a time?

How would you compare listening to these pieces with your listening to and experiencing God?

How might you be able to 'listen' to God with your whole body as mentioned earlier?

In today's passage the word 'listen' is used in the Infinitive Absolute,[78] a form of the infinitive of a verb that has the purpose of intensifying it. It is the equivalent of underlining something in a red marker, making sure it is noticed and paid due attention. It is as though God is saying, 'instead of *hearing* Me, why not *really listen* to Me?'

---

[77] Oliveros, *Deep Listening*, xxv.

[78] In biblical Hebrew the precise function of the *qal* Infinitive Absolute is still being debated by grammarians. That said, one of the known uses of the qIA is when it is found in conjunction with a finite verb of the same root. In such cases the qIA seems to underscore or reinforce the meaning of the finite verb and is usually translated as 'surely' or 'indeed'. In other words, it can be noticed because the verb will appear twice in a row, in this case it would roughly be: "Listen listen to Me..." Some other examples include: "... If a man would give for love all the wealth of his house, it would be <u>despised</u>." Song of Songs 8:6. "<u>Really</u>, is My arm too short that it cannot redeem?" Isaiah 50:2. For more information on the qAI (p. 221) or other aspects of biblical Hebrew I recommend Dr Lily Kahn, *The Routledge Introductory Course in Biblical Hebrew* (London: Routledge, 2014).

Spend a few moments quietly considering both parts of the passage...

«Why do you spend money for what is not bread, and work for that which does not satisfy?

What is 'what is not bread' for you? What might you be spending time on that is not leaving you truly satisfied or satiated?
<u>*Listen*</u> *to Me, and eat what is good, and let your soul delight in abundance.»*

*   *   *

Below are some questions from composer Pauline Oliveros you might like to engage some other time, questions that will help develop your listening skills, increase your awareness of sound and positively impact your awareness of God.[79]

- o   Are you listening now?
- o   What sounds remind you of home?
- o   When do you feel sound in your body?
- o   Do you remember the last sound you heard before you read this question?
- o   How many sounds can you hear all at once?
- o   What are you hearing right now? How is it changing?
- o   How far away can you hear sounds?
- o   If you could hear any sound you wanted, what would it be?
- o   Are you listening to sounds right now or just hearing them?
- o   What sound is most meaningful to you?
- o   How long can you listen?
- o   Try not listening to anything. What happens?
- o   How can you not listen if your ears never close?
- o   What is your favourite sound? How is it made? When can you hear it? Are you hearing it now?
- o   What sound fascinates you?
- o   What sound makes you speculative?

---

[79] Here is the reference again: Pauline Oliveros, *Deep Listening: A Composer's Sound Practice* (Lincoln, NE: Deep Listening Publications, 2005), 55-56.

Belinda É. Samari

- o   What sound gives you the chills?
- o   What sound ruffles your scalp?
- o   What sound changes your breathing?
- o   What sound would you like whispered in your ear?

Your prayer:

DAY 20
Last words

«A single man of you would put a thousand to flight, for YHVH is fighting for you, as He promised you. For your own sakes, therefore, be most mindful to love YHVH your God. For should you turn away and attach yourselves to the remnant of those nations – to those that are left among you – and intermarry with them, you joining them and they joining you, know for certain that YHVH your God will not continue to drive these nations out before you; they shall become a snare and a trap for you, a scourge to your sides and thorns in your eyes, until you perish from this good land that YHVH your God has given you. I am now going the way of all the earth. Acknowledge with all your heart that not one of the good things that YHVH your God promised you has failed to happen; they have all come true for you, not a single one has failed.» Joshua 23:10-14

"I'm bored of it all" – that is what Sir Winston Churchill is reported to have said as his last words. The words of the dying are considered meaningful, or at least interesting, to those continuing on with life. It seems the rationale is that those nearing the end of their life will utter meaningful thoughts, perhaps more meaningful than the many other thoughts they uttered during their lifetime (though Sir Winston's example might not be quite exemplary in that case). This notion is so common in our culture that a book has been written on people's last words, a 'dictionary of deathbed quotations' from athletes and artists, scientists and soldiers, popes and musicians and many more.[80]

Joshua, the leader of Israel, though perhaps not literally on his deathbed, has grown very old indeed so he summons the commanders, magistrates and officials of Israel to meet with him. Imagine you are coming to the meeting too… Rushing as you are, still you are late and Joshua is already speaking as you sneak in the back hoping to go unnoticed. You have missed the beginning of his speech but nevertheless you listen intently.

---

[80] C. Bernard Ruffin, *Last Words: A Dictionary of Deathbed Quotations*, (Jefferson, NC: McFarland & company, 2006).

After the meeting is over and all is said and done, it seems that what you did manage to hear was perhaps the main point and you are glad you came when you did.

In his speech Joshua reminds the Israelites of what God has done for them so far and of the promise God has given to them. Because He is faithful to that promise, God will do all that is necessary to create the conditions for its fulfilment from His side. Yet while encouraging them to keep on, Joshua gives them a heads up, as it were, on where the traps lie and what the weak spot could be that leads to their demise. Joshua's last words: encouragement of what to pursue coupled with a word of caution.

Note the following five things from today's text…

o   *God fights for you*, you are not alone, God is on your side (23:10)

Widows, orphans, refugees, trafficking victims – the list of those left by the wayside without anyone to fight for them is sadly much too long. Have you ever wanted someone to stand up for you, to defend you and support you when you were in the thick of it? When life gets hard and we are afraid and vulnerable we want to know we are not alone, we need someone to have our back, no matter what. You are not alone, God has your back; He is passionately fighting for you and wants to remind you of that, to put your mind at ease and let you know He is right there with you.

o   *He made a promise*, He is reliable (23:10)

This echoes the message from DAY 14: God's promise is rock solid, He can be relied on, He can be counted on and taken at His word. Not only does God fight for you, He really, really means it. Many promise to be there when we need them most but when the situation arises, too often we are left standing on our own. But God's words are more than syllables clumped together, His intention is embedded in His promise and He will come through for you, no doubt about it.[81]

---

[81]   "A lie for a Hebrew is not as it is for us, a non-agreement with the truth […] for him the lie is the internal decay and destruction of the word (*dabar*, דָּבָר)[…] that which is powerless, empty and vain is a lie: a spring which gives no water lies (Isaiah 58:11)." The word in this passage translated as 'fail (not)' is כָּזַב, *khazav*, which means

o   *Choose carefully and choose wisely* (23:12)

Joshua is discouraging his people from 'attaching themselves' to the nations surrounding them. The word 'attach' or 'cling to' (*dabaq*, דָּבַק) is the same word used in Genesis 2:24 when talking of a husband and wife 'sticking' to each other when they marry.[82] The message is to be careful who you are 'marrying', be wise about who you are letting yourself get close to, who you are giving your heart to, who you are joining your life with and building a future with. Be wise about who you are 'sticking' to, because this will impact you profoundly.

o   *God's word is 100% reliable* (23:13)

The phrase 'know for certain…' is in the *qal* Infinitive Absolute, which you learnt about just yesterday. God's advice is: do not cling to those surrounding you, but if you do, when things get ugly, I will not just drive them away and make all your problems disappear and not because I do not love you. If you choose so you can be sure that you will then have to live with them and experience the consequences of your choice, 'pain as thorns in flesh and traps and sores'. Joshua is relaying the warning to them while they have not yet made a choice and can make an informed decision.

o   *Fulfilment is guaranteed* (23:14)

Joshua is reminding the people that what God said came true. Whether it be a promise or a warning, if God says it, it will happen. Though this notion might make us feel a little uncomfortable, especially when words of caution or warning are involved, the fact that God is consistent and reliable can be comforting.

---

to lie, deceive, to be a liar. *Dabar*, 'word', comprises all Hebraic realities: word, deed and concrete object. Boman, *Hebrew Thought Compared to Greek*, 56.
[82] *Dabaq* (דָּבַק) means to cleave closely, adhere to, to be glued together side by side. The image has also been described as the melting of two metals into one; once they are joined, to separate them one from the other is impossible.

Go back and skim through the five points above. Which of these five things speaks to you the most today, which ones seems to reach out to you more than the others? When you have identified it, slowly read that section again.

Now if you narrow it down to a sentence within that section, which one would you single out as the one that captures you most?

Sifting through that sentence, what is the phrase or word that resonates the most with you?

Note down this section, sentence or phrase/word in your notebook (even the order or section-sentence-phrase/word)...

Read through today's Biblical passage bearing in mind your keyword or phrase that you have identified... What do you notice?

What associations are surfacing?

What images, memories or thoughts are you noticing?

What seems to be the core message for you today?

In what ways does this relate to your life at the moment?

Take a moment to bring your inner chatter to a simmer... In the quiet, eyes closed and completely relaxed, imagine you have in front of you two pairs of (eye) glasses... One pair is *'encouragement'* and the other is *'caution'*... Look at both pairs... Now take one pair and put them on... Notice how it feels to wear them... As you do, imagine that through them you are looking at yourself and your life... Notice what you see... Spend as much time looking as you feel you need to and when you are ready, without any rush, move on to the next pair of glasses... When you feel you have spent enough time, slowly bring your attention back to the room and read on below...

*   *   *

Using your drawing materials, draw what you saw through each pair of glasses...

*   *   *

How would you describe the pairs of glasses?

Which pair of glasses did you put on first?

How did you feel as you looked through each pair of glasses?

What did you see?

Which image did you draw first ('encouragement' or 'caution')?

How do your two images differ? Are they similar in any way?

Looking at your images for both, are there any other nuances you might be noticing? What might your images be telling you?

What messages of encouragement might you be able to notice?

Is there anything God might be trying to warn you about?

Are you open to hearing both aspects of His message to you?

What reactions do each of these stir within you?

Consider what you have drawn in connection with what you singled out as the core message or keyword/phrase from the five points mentioned earlier... Write down your observations in your notebook...

Your prayer:

DAY 21
the wilderness

«But as for you, turn around and set out for the wilderness by the way of the Red Sea.'

Then you replied to me, saying, 'We have sinned against YHVH; we will indeed go up and fight, just as YHVH our God commanded us.' And every man of you girded on his weapons of war, and regarded it as easy to go up into the hill country.

And YHVH said to me, 'Say to them, "Do not go up and do not fight, for I am not among you; otherwise you will be defeated before your enemies."

So I spoke to you, but you would not listen. Instead you rebelled against the command of YHVH, and acted presumptuously and went up into the hill country.

The Amorites who lived in that hill country came out against you and chased you as bees do, and crushed you from Seir to Hormah."

Then you returned and wept before YHVH; but YHVH did not listen to your voice nor give ear to you.» Deuteronomy 1:40-45

It has been a few months since the Israelites were miraculously freed from enslavement in Egypt. They have survived in the wilderness with God leading and providing for them. All the while He has kept reminding them of His promise to lead them to a place where they will finally be able to live more fully and have a life of freedom, a place that He has prepared just for them. Now, months later, they finally reach the border of Canaan, the promised place. Peering into it as though through a large gate they shrink back in fear, for that land was not without its obstacles or challenges. Terrified, they doubt God and His ability to protect and help them even though He has done nothing but that since He rescued them. They rationalise and back-paddle, finding ways of avoiding going forward. All right, says God, if that is what you want, then *"turn around and set out for the wilderness by the way of the Red Sea."* This is where we pick up the story.

Suddenly they realise they have made a mistake. They were foolish to doubt God and choke on their fears so they try to remedy the situation by doing exactly what God told them *not* to do. They now want to fight the Amorites on their own even though God says 'don't go, I won't be with you, it's not wise, stay where you are or you'll get chased away like bees.' But they go nevertheless, get defeated just as they were told they would be, and they now have to set out into the wilderness.

A new phase begins that will involve trudging through the wilderness for forty years before their descendants come full circle to the border of Canaan and will finally enter that promised place. Some of us are able and ready to plunge into the unknown more easily than others. Sometimes it depends on the circumstances and though we would like to be courageous, often we are just not ready to go that step further, so we need to grow a little more before we can brave unchartered territory.

That is just a quick overview of the context of today's passage. Rather than focusing on the big picture today, zoom in on that first sentence that changes the course of their lives, the road into the wilderness. Whether it be plan A or plan B is irrelevant, but the wilderness will prove to be an invaluable experience.

From where you are now, turn and face the road; look at it, mark it, prepare for it. Pull up your tent pins, uproot anything that holds you back, holds you firmly in one place, where you are comfortable, and start your journey, be on your way. Your journey is into the wilderness, the desert; a vast, open field in which I will be able to direct and guide you. When you are there, listen for My voice.

Draw lines on a piece of paper to divide it into six equally sized spaces. Number each space in the corner so that you can keep easier track of what you need to draw in each one.

1	2	3
4	5	6

Inspired by the theme of a journey into the wilderness, draw a fictional story containing the six elements below.[83] Begin from space 1 and work your way through, being sensitive to what is going on inside you... For example if you feel you need to draw in 1 and 2 and then 5 or 6 and then work backwards, follow your intuition... The most important thing is that you are not thinking this through, but rather allowing the story to unfold and it will if you let it... Even as you read through the instructions below, allow your mind to be free and not linger and plan ahead regarding any aspect of the story. Briefly read the instructions then put them aside and begin with your story... Go with whatever comes even if it seems strange; let your imagination run free...

1. *the main character in a setting* (this need not be a human, it can be an animal, a supernatural being or a talking flowerpot, but there has to be something with some sort of a life form, or will, or some sense of being alive)
2. *a task for the main character* (this is perhaps a journey to be made, an enemy to be defeated, something to be built, a lost object to be found...)
3. *obstacles in the main character's way* (these factors will oppose the main character, these may be weaknesses or inabilities that the main character possesses; they could be objects, weapons, things found in the environment; or they may be enemies who will attack and try to thwart the main character...)
4. *things that help the main character* (these are things that will make the main character likely to succeed; they could be internal things, externally passive or externally active forces, objects, other characters, qualities, abilities...)
5. *the climax or main action of the story* (this is the main action of the story, the crucial turning point where we see how and whether the main character achieves their task...)

---

[83] The Six-Part Story Method (6PSM) fully described by its originators by M. Lahad and O. Ayalon, BASIC Ph - The story of coping resources, *Community stress prevention*, Vol. II., (Kiryat Shmona, Israel: Community Stress Prevention Centre, 1993).

6. *the consequences or aftermath of the story* (What next? What happens after the main action?)

*   *   *

How did you feel as you were filling in the spaces, revealing the story? Does anything come to mind, did you notice anything along the way? If so, make a note of it in your journal...

Take a few moments to soak in what you have drawn...

Where on the page are your eyes, what are you noticing?

What is it that is capturing your attention?

With all of these questions (which are, as usual, intended to trigger other questions for you to explore), imagine that sitting beside you is an inquisitive child who is asking you about your story. Imagine what kind of questions they would ask and then answer them...

Describe your main character in a few sentences...

What does your description tell you, what do those attributes say about the main character?

How do those attributes relate to the story?

Would you say they were part of the background information, or perhaps more directly relevant to the plot?

How does the main character feel about the task that lies ahead (be generous with your adjectives)?

Is it something the character has done before, or perhaps never done?

Has the main character chosen this task or is it something they have somehow found themselves in through some particular circumstances?

Looking over each of the six spaces, which space was the easiest to fill? Why?

Which was the most difficult?

Which were easier to identify and depict, the obstacles (3) or the things that helped (4)? Why?

It might not be the case, but is there perhaps a connection between what you found easiest/most difficult with that you find easiest/most difficult in real life? For example you might usually be clear on the 'character' or the 'task' but less clear on how it is going to be accomplished; or perhaps you are clear on what the obstacles are but not so clear on what will help... It

117

is interesting to simply notice and observe whether there are any common threads and what they might be...

What are the obstacles you are facing right now?

How about the things that are helping you along the way, are you able to recognise what they are?

How do these elements from the story relate to where you are now in your life?

Be clear about the connection before you move on...

The turning point, the peak of the story, what does it look like? Notice all the senses...

If you were to step into that scene, what would you hear, smell, see... What is happening? How does the character fit into that scene, what is his/her/its role?

What is the general mood in this part of the story?

After the main action is over and done with, what follows?

What fills the sixth space?

How does the main character feel about it?

Which emotion fills this space?

Coming back to our theme for today, how is the wilderness interwoven into your story? Is it part of the setting, a backdrop to any of the scenes along the way?

Which elements of the wilderness (whether literal or symbolic) can you trace in your story?[84]

Taking a sweeping glance at your entire story, which space are you in right now, are you in the midst of a particular scene?

When you have recognised that place, acknowledge that you are there...

---

[84] You may want to explore your story through another lens. For example, 'sound'. Imagine a radar that registers sound levels; as each space (1-6) would be 'scanned' by this radar, what would be the sound levels in each space, in each section of the story? Which part is the loudest, which the softest? What kind of sounds are they? Human voices, talking, singing, sounds from nature or machinery, pleasant, unpleasant...? Does this have any bearing on the plot of the story? You may want to do this with any other element (not just sound) that may come to mind.

What is that scene communicating to you, what is it offering?
Notice how it feels to be in that space and what it means to you...

*   *   *

Each of us has a story to tell. In fact yours and mine is a story that consists of many smaller stories. Each new day is a story in itself (and not even the smallest of stories) and yet even our life in its entirety is not the largest story being told. Some of us will be led into the literal wilderness as part of our life's journey, and some of us will share the essence of the wilderness experience without ever setting foot in one. Either way, the wilderness experience has its place in our life's story.

«You finally realize that the void is yourself. It is like some huge mirror for your mind. Clean and uncluttered, it is the opposite of our urban distractive spaces. Out here, the unbound mind can run free. Space becomes a projection screen. Inside becomes outside. *You can see what you are.*» - Bill Viola (emphasis added)

For me this quote above articulates the essence of the wilderness experience - a place of heightened awareness from which profound changes ensue.

Here is the paraphrase of this text once again:

From where you are now, turn and face the road; look at it, mark it, prepare for it. Pull up your tent pins, uproot anything that holds you back, holds you firmly in one place, where you are comfortable, and start your journey, be on your way. Your journey is into the wilderness, the desert; a vast, open field in which I will be able to direct and guide you. When you are there, listen for My voice.

And the message is simply:
Start your journey (let go of anything holding you back)
Let God fight for you
Make Him the centre of your life (listen)

Your prayer:

DAY 22
choice

«However, the high places were not removed; as yet, the people had not directed their hearts toward the God of their fathers.» 2 Chronicles 20:33

Idolatry. Seems like such an old-fashioned word, so passé, does it not? Shrines, sacrifices, offerings, it is all so ancient. What does idolatry even mean and who today considers themselves an idolater or idolatress? But then there is author Timothy Keller whose book *Counterfeit Gods* makes one stop and wonder: is there still such a thing as idolatry in the 21st century?

«A counterfeit god is anything so central and essential to your life that, should you lose it, your life would hardly feel worth living. An idol has such a controlling position in your heart that you can spend most of your passion and energy, your emotional and financial resources, on it without a second thought.»[85]

"Me? No, I don't have anything in my life that controls me like that, that almost sounds scary; no, I have my faults, yes, but overall I'd say I'm pretty balanced…" I would not be surprised if your first reaction upon reading that last statement was something like that. Yet Keller states that the biblical concept of idolatry is an extremely sophisticated idea, integrating intellectual, psychological, social, cultural, and spiritual categories, something to which we 21st century world-citizens are not immune.

If you still have your doubts, take a look at some of the things Keller lists as our modern-day idols:

o peer approval
o romantic love
o 'saving face'

---

[85] Timothy Keller, *Counterfeit Gods: When the Empty Promises of Love, Money and Power Let You Down*, (Place: Hodder & Stoughton, 2010).

o   access to certain social circles

o   career

o   family

o   emotional dependence of others on you

o   your intellect

o   health, fitness and physical beauty

o   individual freedom

o   self-discovery

o   personal affluence and fulfilment

o   competence and skill

o   a great political or social cause

o   moral virtue

'Idols?', you say, 'These things, really?' Contrary to what our initial associations with idols might be, the things in the list above are, perhaps surprisingly, all good things. None of them are 'wrong' or 'bad' *per se*, yet therein lies the paradox. As Keller explains, the problem is that

«[…] The human heart takes good things like a successful career, love, material possessions, even family, and turns them into ultimate things. Our hearts deify them as the centre of our lives, because, we think, they can give us the significance and security, safety and fulfilment, if we attain them.»[86]

He also says that:

«We may not physically kneel before the statue of Aphrodite, but many young women today are driven into depression and eating disorders by an obsessive concern over their body image. We may not actually burn incense to Artemis, but when money and career are raised to cosmic proportions, we perform a kind of child sacrifice, neglecting family and community to achieve a higher place in business and gain more wealth and prestige.»[87]

«There are idols everywhere.» (emphasis added)

---

[86]   Keller, Counterfeit Gods, xiv.
[87]   Keller, *Counterfeit Gods*, xii.

This begs the question: What are your idols?[88] As I said, our first reaction might be one of protest, that we do not have any, but as Keller says:

«I am not asking whether or not you have rival gods. I assume that we all do; they are hidden in every one of us... »[89]

Idolatry was a common occurrence in the history of Israel and its emergence was usually connected to whoever was the ruler at that time.

The book of Chronicles is known for its exhaustive lists of the kings of Israel and Judah. King after king is listed and described, most often without much elaboration, the crux of his reign summarised in a punch line: he did what was evil in God's sight, or, he did what was right and good. Ultimately it boiled down to that. Much like a conductor, who greatly determines the sound of the orchestra both personally and musically, a leader influences those who follow him or her. A good king meant that, for the most part, the people did good, too. Equally so, a king who did evil meant those over whom he reigned were more likely to follow in his footsteps.

In the passage leading up to today's text, a good king is mentioned, one that did not turn away from doing good all his life. Yet right after saying that, the author says, ah yes, but the high places or shrines dedicated to other gods still dotted the landscape and as for the people, they had not fully turned their hearts to God. A leader can only go so far. Even a good king does not guarantee a 'perfect' nation, and the choice to live one way or another is always down to each individual.

The text literally says the Israelites had not as yet prepared their hearts… The word 'prepared' is the Hebrew word *kun* (כּוּן) meaning to *be firm, to set up, establish (lit. or fig.), prepare, determine, confirm, direct, be stable, order, make provision…* In today's context *kun* refers to the established, stable part of the day, i.e. midday, when the sun seems motionless in mid-heaven.

In other words, the Israelites had not yet set their heart on God,

---

[88] Keller mentions several ways we can identify what our idols are, by examining: our imagination ('the true god of your heart it what your thoughts effortlessly go to when there is nothing else demanding your attention.'), at how we spend our money ('Your money flows most effortlessly toward your heart's greatest love.'), and also our 'most uncontrollable emotions' ('Do I feel that I *must* have this thing to be fulfilled and significant?'). He adds: "[…] when you pull your emotions up by the roots, you will often find your idols clinging to them.". Keller, *Counterfeit Gods*, 167-170.
[89] Keller, *Counterfeit Gods*, 167.

firmly, without wavering (like the midday sun). They were not stable and determined in their devotion to Him. Even today we have the expression 'to have your heart set on something', conveying the same sentiment of committed devotion.

A player on the court who is for some reason sneaking glances into the crowd and not focusing on the game will be weakened and ineffective. Eventually such a player will greatly incapacitate their entire team. So it is with us; we get distracted by our gods, letting them take prime position in our heart, which in turn renders us incapable of fully setting it on God instead. That is why remembering is important – the more we remember how we have walked with God in the past, the more aware we become of our inner allegiances. The more aware we are, the more difficult it is for us to leave Him for something of less worth.

Danish philosopher Søren Kierkegaard talked about choice and the differences between them: some are determined wholly by the external and immediate, others emanate from within. People often make choices based on external, changing, immediate determinants and thereby think they are avoiding the more difficult (which he calls 'absolute') choices. However the truth is that we do not avoid them. There is never a situation in which we do not make a choice because even choosing not to choose is still a choice. And why is that so? Because as he so eloquently says: *choice is a ubiquitous condition of life*. In other words, choice is unavoidable; it permeates every aspect of our lives.

Ensure that you are in a quiet space where you will be undisturbed... Gently closing your eyes, focus your attention on your breath and just breathe for a few moments, quieting your self-talk... When you feel you are ready, read the following paragraph to imagine a place. After spending as much time in that place as you feel you need to, portray your experience on paper in any way you wish...

Imagine you are walking through the corridor of a large building...

There are many corridors... many times you reach a split and can turn left or right, you go down many flights of stairs...

You now reach the end of a corridor and see a door... you open it...

You step into in a room or space... you look around and something catches your eye... Two chairs... one of them is yours...

Notice what they are like...
How does it feel to be in that space?
What can you hear, smell, touch?

*   *   *

Now that you have portrayed your experience in whatever way you felt best, reflect on your experience in that imaginary place... Remember, these questions are intended to be a guide for questions that may arise that I have not written down... You will perhaps feel a pull toward a certain aspect of the story or scenes; follow that trusting your intuition...

How was it being in the corridors?
How did it feel having to choose to turn left or right?
How about descending down the flights of stairs, what was going through your mind?
Once you stepped into the room/space, how did it initially feel? What did you see? What could you hear, smell and touch?

Reflecting on the two chairs you saw, how would you describe them?
Where were they situated in the space (far apart, close, facing each other, etc.)?
What did they look like?
How would you describe your chair, the one you knew belonged to you?
Did you interact with the chairs (observe, sit on them, walk around...)
Be as descriptive as you can, noting down anything that comes to mind... Be sensitive to any insights based on what you are noticing...

*   *   *

Consider the choices you have made today or have to make today... the choices you have made in the past week, month, year...
Which were relatively easy?
Which were difficult?
Were there some extremely difficult choices you were faced with?
Are you facing such a choice right now?

You may choose to do this now or come back to it at some later time, but go back and comb through Keller's list of gods again, carefully and without rushing... Without thinking, sit with the list and observe what comes to the surface...

*   *   *

Whatever our counterfeit gods may be and as difficult as it may be to admit it, we willingly *choose* them, consciously or unconsciously we allow them to reign supreme in our hearts. Recognising our idols is an important step and yet only half of the task – the other half is to then willingly *choose* to change the order of things within our heart, to allow ourselves to be internally restructured and make the choice to firmly set our heart on God. Admittedly this is all easier said than done, but it is real and it is possible.

«Creation is possible only if there is choice. And choice is only possible if there is freedom.» Leonard Meyer

The quote above mentions these terms in the following order: creation – choice – freedom. Working backwards through the quote one could say: we are free therefore we can choose, hence we can create.

Your prayer:

DAY 23

essence => healing

«*For most of the people – many from Ephraim and Manasseh, Issachar and Zebulun – had not purified themselves, yet they ate the Passover sacrifice violating what was written. Hezekiah prayed for them, saying, 'The good YHVH will provide atonement for everyone who set his heart on worshiping God, YHVH God of his fathers, even if he is not purified for the sanctuary. YHVH carefully listened to Hezekiah and healed the people.*»
2 Chronicles 30:18-20

What are some of your favourite rituals? Spaghetti Bolognese every Thursday night, reading the paper with your morning coffee, your nightly routine of make-up-off-cleanser-toner-moisturiser-the-works...? Our rituals can be something we do alone or with others, often or rarely. Whatever it may be, we all have our rituals of one kind or another.

Still in the realm of rituals, in your mind now, flip back to the night the Israelites were delivered from their oppressive slavery in Egypt. It was a miraculous rescue that changed the course of the lives of thousands in that enslaved community. It was a night to be remembered not only by them, but also by countless generations to come. That significant event was celebrated each year in the early Spring[90] in the festival known as *Pesach*, or Passover (it was one of the seven annual festivals of the Israelites). It is at this time of the year that we enter into this unusual episode recorded in today's passage.

The Festival is fast approaching and King Hezekiah calls the people to turn back to God, asking that they not be stubborn, but rather give themselves to God, set their hearts on Him and come to the temple and serve Him. He encourages them by saying that God has given them 'one heart' to do what He commanded them. In other words, God had enabled

---

[90] Beginning in the late afternoon of the fourteenth day of the first month (Nissan) of the year. "[...] the date creates the 'temporal space', or occasion, for rituals to exercise their function." Ithamar Gruenwald, *Rituals and ritual theory in ancient Israel*, (Leiden: Brill, 2012), 10.

them to fully turn to Him if they wanted to. The people are to respond and go and destroy their altars dedicated to other gods, throwing them into the River Kidron. Then they could come earnestly seeking God and take part in the *Pesach* rituals. The only problem is that at this point in the story, they have taken part but they have come unprepared ('had not purified themselves').

You see, there were set rules that were to be followed as a way of preparing oneself for the ritual activities of Passover. They were intended to prepare the whole person for what was about to take place: a sacred remembering of the deliverance from bondage. Without following the prescribed steps as part of their preparation, they were actually not allowed to take part in the festival.

This brings us to the key moment in the story: What now? What will happen to them? Is what they have done not enough? Will they be punished? Will they still be blessed even though they have breached protocol? As scholar Ithamar Gruenwald mentions below, the order of the ritual acts were not trivial in the least, but rather extremely important.

«An important principle of rituals is that the components of the ritual act require an orderly performance. This order establishes the inner logic of the ritual acts. The essential factors, therefore, that are active in shaping rituals, are the detailed prescriptions that should be followed and the notion that not following the prescription means failure, with all the consequences that such a failure entails. In any event, all rituals are conducive to creating desired changes, technically called 'transformations'.»[91]

The prescribed actions involved in preparation for the event were embedded with meaning, not just the event itself. The whole proces of the preparation *and* the 'main event' were intended to facilitate a transformation for those who took part in it.

Realizing what has happened, King Hezekiah turns to God on their behalf, asking Him to acknowledge them and asking Him to participate in the ritual in spite of the unusual circumstances. He asks that God forgive (Hebrew word 'to cover') them, all of them who have come and in essence, have indeed prepared (*kun*) their hearts to seek God. Hezekiah trusts that

---

[91] Gruenwald, *Ritual and ritual theory in ancient Israel*, vii-viii.

even though this time things have not gone according to plan or protocol, as they usually would and should do, God will nevertheless bless them and recognise their earnest desire for Him.

Indeed He does. Knowing the depths of their hearts God covers their impurity and uncleanness. He heals them (*rapha*, see DAY 6) and makes them whole. After all, the purpose of the Passover ritual is to remember how God delivered the earlier generations, to honour that special relationship between them and God, and more than that – it is intended to inspire them to experience the essence of that same freedom and transformation in their own hearts.

The Israelites did not externalise the principle in the prescribed motions, but they *embodied the principle* nonetheless.

In the Hebrew language the word *biyn* (בִּין) (not mentioned in today's text) means to *penetrate to the core*, to discern, to have insight (to dismember, separate), to understand the interaction of the elements involved. For the Israelites it was important to separate the essential from the non-essential and to get to the heart of the matter (notice the English phrase for it!). These people who showed up seeking God, 'unprepared' by certain standards, had aligned themselves with God in keeping with the essence of the festival. They had understood its core in their hearts.

You do not have to have it all figured out, and you may not be where you want to be, or as far along as you would like to be. But having the *right attitude* makes *all the difference*. The rest follows much more easily. God honours an open, earnest heart – why not start there?

*Embody the principle.

De-cluttering

The Israelites had not done all that was set out by protocol, but they did do something: they threw away their altars, the things they knew needed letting of in order for them to be able to move forward.

What is preventing you from moving forward?

If you were on the banks of the River Kidron with them that day, what would you be throwing into the water?

Are you aware of the things that are not beneficial for you?

Draw a rubbish skip (trash can, big black hole, whatever you wish) in which you are about to throw all the things that are clogging up your life and holding you back. If you like, gather stones from your surrounding, write one thing on each stone and then go outside and throw them away (perhaps in a lake, river or the ocean), one by one, really letting them go.

*　　　*　　　*

Attitude of the heart

Plainly said: they got the point. Yes, they breached protocol, but nevertheless they understood the core of what was going on. They showed up fully in their 'incompleteness' and God honoured that.

I once heard of a tale of two people who had both lost a leg in some sort of an accident. One was in a wheelchair, depressed and suicidal. The other was also in a wheelchair but was a cheerful advocate for those with missing limbs; the same external situation, but completely different attitudes.

Honestly speaking, what is the attitude of your heart right now?

To which person are you more similar? Why might that be?

*　　　*　　　*

Healing

The reason why the Israelites had come to participate in this significant event was, among other things, to be blessed, to be healed and to be renewed.

Flip back to DAY 6. Look at your drawings and what you wrote down as answers to the exercises.

Has anything changed since then?

How is progress noticeable?

Has the notion of 'healing' changed for you at all?

How do you feel knowing that God can and will heal you even if you still have not got it all solved and sorted out?

Your prayer:

DAY 24
crossroads

«[...] Stand by the roads and consider, inquire about ancient paths: which is the road to happiness? Travel it, and find tranquillity for yourselves [...]»
Jeremiah 6:16

After being unemployed for what seems like an eternity you now have two job offers. Both are appealing but you are stressed because you are wondering: Which way do I go? You graduate and now you can travel the world for a year or immediately continue on with your studies; which way do you go? You get the idea – crossroads one after the other. Feel free to add your own examples here, I know you have plenty of them.

On DAY 22 we explored 'choice' and were reminded that the act of choosing is inevitable in life. Sometimes we welcome the opportunity to choose from multiple options whilst other times we run and hide, squiggle and squirm, all to avoid it (I imagine a protesting child clamming its mouth shut while its mother tries to get it to eat a spoonful of mush).

Crossroads.
A criss-cross of paths where choices must be faced and decisions must be made.
Not always a walk in the park.

Broken down to its essence based on the Hebrew text, today's passage advises:
Stand by the road of your life. Be fully present and dwell on how you live it. Consider it, really look at it with discernment, experience it. Then ask, request, even demand in an earnest way, wish for, consult God about the eternal path, the one that is smaller than the big roads, the one that is travelled by foot, the one that is more often than not, veiled from sight. Ask where the good way is for you. Then, travel it, walk it, grow in it, prosper, pursue it and take the journey. When you do, your soul, the very life within you, will suddenly find a resting place. You will suddenly go from a state of being tossed about, of questioning

and confusion, to a state of quiet, calm and rest. Things will break, and divide, but will suddenly and unexpectedly give you rest.

If we take the above, deconstruct it and view it as steps of a type of 'decision-making template', it might look like something this:

Consider/
discern/
reflect => ask/
        require => **(blank)** => travel/
                                 walk/
                               move forward => find/
                                                peace/
                                                calm/
                                                rest

Looking at the sequence of steps it seems that the actual revelatory moment, a vital step in this progression, is left unsaid and unpacked. It seems that that blank space is precisely where God answers us and reveals the path to us. Without this component the second half of the template cannot happen. Until we are enlightened and confident of the way in which to go, we remain in the place of enquiring and waiting. Undeniably, the key component in the middle – the revelation of God's path for us – puts everything else into motion.

Go back and carefully read the paraphrase of this verse. What images does it inspire?

Notice words that might feel stronger as you read through it again, anything that might 'tug' at you while you are reading it...

Before moving on to the creative exercise, prepare a pen or pencil and your notebook or pieces of paper that you will be ready to use when the time comes.

Find a quiet place where you will be undisturbed... Stand in the middle of your room (or wherever you are) and close your eyes... In your mind, imagine you are at a crossroads... Take a few moments to just breathe and place yourself in that imaginary place... With your eyes closed, turn your head as you 'look' around you, soaking in what you can see, hear, smell...

Notice how your feet feel on the ground... As you are standing there, ask yourself these questions and notice what the answers might be... Where was I before I came to this crossroads? Why am I here now? Where am I going? How do I feel being here? What am I afraid of? What am I hoping for? What am I expecting? Notice these things and any others that may arise as you stand there with eyes closed, really immersing yourself in this imaginary place... When you feel you have spent enough time there, slowly open your eyes and, without any hesitation, take a pencil and paper, and journal for approximately 10-15 minutes (do not worry about grammar or sentence structure, etc.).

*   *   *

How did the journaling feel after being at the crossroads, how was the transition from images to words? What did you put down on paper? Did you write about how it felt to be at the crossroads, did you perhaps write about a real life situation, a memory that surfaced? Does what you wrote seem coherent or does it resemble a free flow of thoughts?

Take a few moments now and reflect on how it felt to be at the crossroads in your imagination... As you stood there, what was going through your mind? How did you feel (identify the emotion/s)? What kind of a place was it, describe the setting... Note down everything you noticed whilst in that place, remember that these are only questions to guide you, not having answers to them is all right as each person's experience will be unique (e.g. what you were wearing, what time of day or year it was, answers to questions mentioned before: why are you at the crossroads, where are you headed, where did you come from, what are you hoping for, etc.).

Once you have done that, read through what you wrote and consider it in connection to your crossroads imagery... Do you see a similar thread, do they seem to be part of the same thing or are you perhaps a little puzzled about what you wrote? Note down your impressions about this...

*   *   *

Consider the crossroads on your life's path as you glance backwards... when were you at a crossroads in your life? How many times have you felt you were at a significant crossroads? (Bear in mind that often we reach inner crossroads, where there is a tumult and upheaval, a deep stirring within us whilst our outer circumstances may remain unchanged). What were the paths that lay before you and which one did you take? Do the crossroads in your past have any similarities between them? How would you describe the way in which you usually face the crossroads to which you come? What, if anything, might you be noticing about that?

Remember:
Consider/discern
Path vs. road
Divide/break
The good path is often hidden from plain sight
Ask!
Journey (travel)
Rest

Your prayer:

DAY 25

time

«To everything there is a season, a time for every experience under heaven. A time for being born and a time for dying, a time for planting and a time for uprooting the planted, a time for killing and a time for healing, a time for tearing down and a time for building up, a time for weeping and a time for laughing, a time for wailing and a time for dancing, a time for throwing stones and a time for gathering stones, a time for embracing and a time for refraining from embracing, a time for seeking and a time for losing, a time for keeping and a time for discarding, a time for ripping and a time for sewing, a time for silence and a time for speaking, a time for loving and a time for hating, a time for war and a time for peace [...] He makes everything beautiful in its time [...]» Ecclesiastes 3:1-8,11a

Before we take a further step into today's passage we need to talk about 'time'. This word is repeated over again in the passage above and it seems crucial that we come to a closer understanding of it as it is presented in the text. Language, thought and culture are interwoven and generally we do not need convincing of this, even when it comes to time. The Africans even have an affectionate saying: 'The Europeans have watchers, the Africans have time!' On a more serious note, Lera Boroditsky investigated whether language shapes thought by comparing Mandarin and English speakers' conceptions of time. Without going into the details of the study here, she found that "one's native language appears to exert a strong influence over how one thinks about abstract domains like time."[92] Whilst this can be observed today for contemporary languages, the same has also been asserted for ancient societies and cultures. Numerous studies of the ancient Near East reveal that cultures in antiquity, such as that of the ancient Israelites, had differing views amongst themselves, but also differing from our own Western perspectives today. These views concern all sorts of

---

[92] Lera Boroditsky. "Does Language Shape Thought?: Mandarin and English Speakers' Conceptions of Time", *Cognitive Psychology* 43 (2001), 1-22, quote on p. 18.

aspects of human life, from the way we understand what the human being is, to how we conceptualise calendars and time.[93]

Consider the two different perspectives as you now imagine you are in conversation with someone from the West (imagine a European) and an ancient Israelite, both of whom are telling you their understanding of 'time'. It might go something like this. [94]

European: Time…hm… Well, immediately I think of myself at a given point on a time-line with my face pointed forward. Where I am standing right now is the *present*, today or now. Before me lies the *future* and behind me is the *past* (and I speak in past, present and future tenses). The past is defined with reference to an objective point on the time-line (it's behind me on the line); the future still lies before me and its effect has not yet been carried out in relation to where I am at the moment (it is further along on the time-line). For me time is something abstract and it is separate from the events that occur in it.

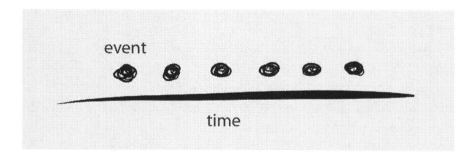

Israelite: Well…When I consider time, the first thing that comes to mind is an *event*. For me time is determined by its content, by what happens. In other words, time is a stream of events. Within that stream there can be two types of events: those that are *complete* and those that are *incomplete* (and my language reflects complete and incomplete actions). When I say 'complete' that means that from my viewpoint as an experiencing person,

[93] E.g. Dr Ulrike Steinert's book investigates ancient Mesopotamian concepts of the human person. Ulrike Steinert, *Aspekte des Menschseins im Alten Mesopotamien: Eine Studie zu Person und Identität im 2. und 1. Jt. v. Chr.*, Cuneiform Monographs 44, (Leiden: Brill, 2012). For information on the different calendars in antiquity see Sacha Stern, *Calendars in Antiquity*, (Oxford: Oxford University Press, 2012).
[94] Explanations based on Boman, *Hebrew Thought compared with Greek*, chapter 'Time and Space'.

an action has been completed and is now something that is factually before me. The incomplete action also stands in reference to me (not in relation to where it is on an 'objective time-line') and when I talk of the future it does not 'lie before me' but rather 'comes after me' and is something that I regard as continuous, in the process of taking place or newly emerging. For me the emphasis is not on the moment of time but on the situation.

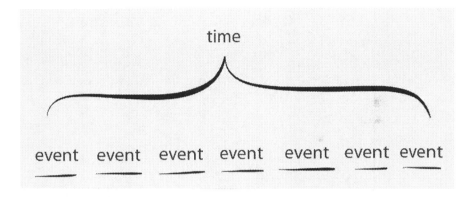

It seems quite obvious that these views are very different from each other. Interestingly enough, in most of the world's languages the original function of the tense-stems of the verb was not that of designating *time* (past-present-future) but of designating *aspect* (kind of action).[95]

To make the ancient Israelite understanding of time as expressed above even clearer, we will examine the Hebrew terms for 'past' and 'future' from which this understanding stems. The Hebrew term *qedem* (קֶדֶם) means the front of a place or time. So for example, it refers to the east (the cardinal direction at the time) and also to past time. The Hebrew term *acharit* (אַחֲרִית) means the last, or end, stemming from the root that means what is behind, hence its meaning of the future. Imagine you are rowing on a river. As you row what you see before you is the past, and what is behind you is the future. The past is clearly seen and the future is unknown.[96]

---

[95] *Ibid.* Henry Welsford neatly expresses it in this way: "In stating that the Hebrew verb has only two tenses, or times, I hardly know whether the circumstance ought to be regarded as an imperfection in words, or a perfection in things; as a defect in grammar, or a superior accuracy in philosophy." Henry Welsford, Esq. *Mithridates Minor; or An Essay on Language*, (London: Longman, Brown, Green and Longmans, 1848), 65.

[96] The river analogy I owe in part to Dr Michael Brown.

Bringing today's passage to the forefront again, go back and read through it again, slowly, trying to process it through the 'lenses' of the ancient Israelite who viewed time differently than you probably do.

«The time of inner life [...] followed its course in rhythms [...] of antitheses which are constantly replacing one another and every pair of which, together with the stages in between, forms a qualitative unity. So is man's life [...] he [the author] mentions only the extremes but he has included with them all the stages in between.»[97]

Life is one and the other and all in between. We cannot always keep, sew, plant and laugh. We need occasions when we throw things away, when we remain silent rather than speak, when we weep… Life is dynamic and this passage portrays life as it truly is.

That said, we often have a tendency to (for all sorts of reasons) pretend we are in a phase that we are actually not in. 'I'm fine', 'It's all under control', we can get quite creative when convincing ourselves, and others, that we are where we *want* to be rather than where we actually *are*. The irony is that unless we are able to be honest about where we are, no matter how uncomfortable or painful that place may be, we cannot move on, we are prolonging the very thing we are doing our best to avoid.

Just for a moment now, consider things that surround you for which the process of time plays a significant role. For example, some people enjoy baking bread; there is nothing quite like the scent of freshly baked bread wafting through the house. When one begins making the bread, one puts the yeast in warm water with a dash of sugar in a bowl and covers it with a damp cloth. All these components (warm water, sugar, damp cloth) help activate the yeast which then bubbles up and that is the cue to add the flour and begin kneading it. But even with all of these components present one does not know how long it will take for the yeast to rise, one cannot set a timer for it. On a hot summer's day it can take only a few minutes. In the winter when it is cold, it can take much longer and even then it is still not like it is in the summer! It is the same process but how long it takes varies and even with all one might know, it is still impossible to predict its course.

Below is a list of the polarities mentioned in today's text. Copy them

---

[97] Boman, *Hebrew Thought Compared with Greek*, 140-141.

into your notebook and once you have done that, go back through each pair and without thinking, draw a dot or mark along each spectrum depicting where you feel you are at the moment (see examples below).

Planting - - - - - - - - - - -*- - - - - Uprooting
Ripping - - *- - - - - - - - - - - - - Sewing

Please remember that it is not about where you *wish* you were, but where you feel you *really are.* Being at any one point along this spectrum is neither 'good' nor 'bad', neither is better or more desirable *per se*, so be free to leave all judgment and criticism aside and be courageous in your honesty.

Being Born -Dying
Planting -Uprooting
Killing- Healing
Tearing down - - - - - - - - - - - - - - - - - - Building up
Weeping - Laughing
Wailing - Dancing
Throwing stones - - - - - - - - - - - - - - - Gathering stones
Embracing - - - - - - - - - - - - - - - - - Refraining from embracing
Seeking - - - - - - - - - - - - - - - - - - - Losing
Keeping - - - - - - - - - - - - - - - - - - - Discarding
Ripping - Sewing
Silence - - - - - - - - - - - - - - - - - - - Speaking
Loving - Hating
War - Peace

*   *   *

Now that you have acknowledged where you are on each of these spectrums, take another look at the list, letting your eyes brush over it ever so generally...

Imagine that they are all a shade of a certain colour...

Some pairs of polarities are stronger in colour while the others are fainter...

Notice if any one pair stands out... Which one is it?

Would you say this is the pair you resonate with the most?

If that pair were a magnet, would you feel its pull the strongest of them all?

Noticing where you have placed your dots, if they were moving, in which direction would each of them be moving?

When you have identified that pair of polarities, consider where you are along the spectrum... Express in a drawing the phase you feel you are in at the moment and yourself along the spectrum, how it feels to be there... When you have finished, allow yourself to sit with your drawing in a few moments of silence before continuing...

*   *   *

Which pair of polarities was it that called out to you the most?

Do the actual words on each end of that spectrum stir up any pictures, memories or associations?

Which words would you use to describe how you feel about where you are along the spectrum?

Observing your artwork, what do you notice?

Write down (or draw) ways in which the process of time relates to you at the moment. Consider God's promise of making things happen exactly when they are supposed to, at the right time, and as a result, being beautiful...

You are on schedule. Keep going. You are not too early and you are also not late, you are right on time. Keep on your journey, and be present in every stage of it, whether it be one end of the spectrum of the other. You are right on time.

Remember:
You (and God) are on schedule
Life is both ends of the spectrum (balance)
Be present where you are

Whichever phase you might be in right now, remember that the *passing of time* (duration) is *not* the key feature of your phase. You will not grow, progress and move forward to the next phase because you were constantly 'looking at your watch' so to speak, but because you were being sensitive to the peculiarities of your situation and what God might have been bringing to your attention. A phase is over when it is *completed*, when whatever needed to happen within it (within you), happened. How long it takes is irrelevant; it could be a day or it could be a year.

«He has made everything beautiful in its time» is virtually synonymous with the idea of God bringing everything to pass exactly at the right time. This notion of beauty stems from the ancient Hebrew understanding of beauty as here expressed:

«That is beautiful, first of all, which accomplishes its definition and fulfils its purpose; when a thing is as it should be, it is beautiful.»[98]

However 'long' it takes, when your situation is resolved, when things change and you move forward, it is because what needed to ripen ripened. It is an organic process that differs from person to person and situation to situation. When it changes and when that something is completed and has fulfilled its purpose, it is beautiful in the fullest sense of the word.

Your prayer:

---

[98] Boman, *Hebrew Thought compared with Greek*, 87.

essence + form

«[...] Abel became a herder of sheep while Cain was a tiller of soil. And it happened in the course of time that Cain brought from the fruit of the soil an offering to YHVH. And Abel too had brought from the choice firstlings of his flock, and YHVH regarded Abel and his offering but He did not regard Cain and his offering, and Cain was very incensed, and his face fell. And YHVH said to Cain: 'Why are you incensed, and why is your face fallen? For whether you offer well, or whether you do not, at the tent flap sin crouches and for you is its longing but you will rule over it' [...]» Genesis 4:2b-7

When I arrived in the deep heart of south Sudan the locals kindly advised me to always take care in zipping the zip on my tent all the way to the bottom. It was rainy season and that meant it was snake season too. If a careless tent occupier left the tent zip a little open, a snake was very likely to slither inside and most often nest itself on the occupier's bed or in a cosy corner of the tent. Once settled, it was certainly a stressful and tricky ordeal trying to get rid of it, at least for most people, including foreigners such as myself. Needless to say I religiously checked and double-checked that my tent zip was shut – I did not want any surprises.

Cain and Abel are two brothers, Abel, the younger, is a shepherd and Cain is an agriculturalist, a 'tiller of the soil'. As was customary in the ancient Near East in antiquity, offerings would be brought to God and so it happens in today's passage. Abel brings the finest animal from his flock as an offering and his brother brings what he has harvested. God considers Abel and accepts his offering; He considers Cain and his offering but does not accept it.

Cain becomes incensed with anger and it is at this point that God engages him in conversation. Strangely enough God does not proceed to explain why He rejected his offering (as we might expect) or give Cain some tips on how to fix *that* problem ('next time bring this and this'), instead He says something completely 'off topic', apples and oranges, it seems.

Ever so wisely God shifts the focus to something unexpected, to another element in the story by saying something along the lines of: Cain, whether you bring this or that isn't so much the issue here today (though we can talk about that another time if you like). Take a look at this for a moment, please just notice this – you've got another, much bigger problem crouching right outside your front door, it has the potential to lead to your demise – that's what I'd like you to pay attention to right now, I just want you to be aware of that.

Interestingly, the Hebrew term here for 'sin' is *chattah* (חַטָּאָה) derived from the root *chata* (חָטָא) meaning 'to miss the mark'. Clark defines it as *'remove from the source of life*, deviate from the path.'[99] It is almost as though God is saying: Cain the point isn't what you think it is, the point is you're *missing the point*.[100]

God knows Cain's problem runs deeper – it was not a matter of fruit or lamb *per se* – and He is lovingly drawing his attention to that. He points to the larger problem which was essentially this: whether you do good or bad (whether you bring a lamb or fruit), sin crouches at the opening (tent flap) to your heart, your inner abode, the place you call home, where you are safe and seek refuge, where you rest and find peace. Your heart is in danger of being corrupted. The tent flap is not sealed shut, it is flapping wide open. It is in danger of becoming compromised and infiltrated and if it does become so, then your safe haven and place of peace, the very core of your being, will be contaminated.

Even though hearing this was probably not pleasant for Cain, God continues by telling him the good news: even though those harmful things and toxic attitudes will always crouch in the same spot, relentlessly, always wanting you, desiring you, luring and pursuing you in a very active way, you can choose: to master or be mastered. The choice is yours.

Patach (פָּתַח) is a root word meaning to 'open wide (lit. or fig.), to loosen, break forth, draw out, unstop…'. It is from the verb *patach* that

---

[99] Matityahu Clark, *Etymological dictionary of Biblical Hebrew: Based on the Commentaries of Rabbi Samson Raphael Hirsch*, (New York, NY: Feldheim Publishers, 1999), 78.

[100] "For the Hebrew, there was an obvious connection between an action and its consequences. Therefore *chatta'th* means not only the evil deed, but also the associated consequences. The deed itself is conceived of as a sphere surrounding the sinner […] The sphere of calamity has its collective effects […] Whenever *chatta'ah* is used, there is always more involved than the consequences of the deed upon the doer; a further divine intervention is always expected." Botterweck & Ringgren, *Theological Dictionary of the Old Testament*, Vol. IV, 312.

we get the noun *petach* (literally an opening or entrance way) which is the word used in today's passage for 'the tent flap' (also known as door in other translations).[101] '*Petach* signifies something that arrives without us even noticing it and it catches us by surprise. It is often unnoticed and suddenly when we lift our eyes up, suddenly it is there.'[102]

Imagine a storyboard with three sequences to it. Designate three spaces in your notebook for the following exercise (a page each or three squares on a page, etc.)

Complete one drawing at a time and go through them in order... It is important that you not let yourself think but that you draw what naturally comes... At the same time, take your time really engaging the tasks... Only move on to the next drawing when you feel you have finished with the one you are working on at that moment... Some might be more elaborate and take longer to process, others may take less time to complete... Follow your natural tempo...

In drawing 1, draw your tent with its flap as open as you feel it is...

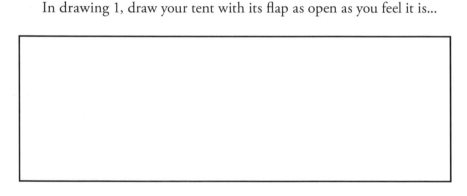

When you have done that, draw (also in the drawing above) the things that are crouching outside your tent flap – what poses a threat to you, what

---

[101] This word is also used elsewhere in the Bible often referring to city gates (commonly *petach sha'ar*; 2 Sam. 11:23, 1 Chr. 19:9; Judges 9:35,40,44). "The actual opening or conduit through the gate is always the strategically critical point in any city's layout." Botterweck & Ringgren, *Theological Dictionary of the Old Testament*, Vol. 12, (Grand Rapids, MI: Wm. B. Eerdmans Publishing Company, 2003), 184. As with a city so with a person's heart, as we notice in today's example.

[102] Boman, *Hebrew Thought Compared with Greek*, 137. "[*petach*] referred first to the concrete opening of a nomad's tent, i.e. to the tent's entrance and exit, and then to any form of opening granting access between 'outside' and 'inside' (or the reverse)." Botterweck & Ringgren, *Theological Dictionary of the Old Testament*, Vol. 12, 174.

is luring you away from God, what makes you afraid, what distracts you and/or harms you in any way...

In drawing 2, draw what you do, what measures you take, to protect yourself from these harmful things just outside your tent flap...

In drawing 3, draw the situation as it is after the previous picture, after you have taken steps to ensure you are safe...

*   *   *

How would you describe the experience of filling in the storyboard? Enjoyable, challenging, slow at first but then it flowed better...?

Take a look at your storyboard...

Which of the three segments draws your attention?

What is it that catches your eye?

Stay there and allow yourself to linger a moment...

Are there any elements in your drawings that catch you by surprise perhaps, or something you perhaps do not understand, not sure of what it is or means?

Would you say there is an overall theme to your story or a general mood?

If you were to give your story a title, what would it be?

As usual, notice your use of colours, look out for any patterns or elements from previous drawings...

What has happened from space 1 to space 3, what is the difference between your two drawings?

Consider for a moment the things that you have drawn outside your tent flap in space 2 – are you able to recognise those things in your life?

How does it feel to acknowledge them there?

Consider each of the three segments, walking your way through the story, as it were, and in silence, stay with and in each segment for as long as you like, giving yourself the space to observe and listen... reflect on how it felt to fill each space... notice what each segment, and the story as a whole, is saying to you...

*   *   *

Reflect on this storyboard you have just drawn... Of all three, only the second drawing is in your control, so to speak. 1 – we cannot control the world we live in, the existence of harmful things, nor can we always control our exposure to them. Equally so, 3 – we do not control the future and we do not always know even vaguely what the outcome will be of some of our actions. But God says the good news is: you decide what to do about the current situation, about right now, today. Make up your mind, ask Me for help, don't be shy, take a stand, and I'll take care of the rest, don't worry about that.

In today's story, God goes to the *essence* of the problem, though the issue is seemingly about the *form*. But essence and form are inextricably bound and God is trying to get that message through to Cain.

Perhaps you have been trying to talk about something with God and He seems to be 'avoiding' the issue or answering in ways that confuse you and seem as though you are getting nowhere... Maybe He is doing what he did with Cain, seemingly going off topic, but in essence addressing something that runs much deeper in you than the issue on the surface… If so, what might it be, what might He be trying to tell you? Spend a few moments with that question…

*   *   *

* The form enables us to better grasp and understand the nature of the essence.

* Adherence to the form reflects inner attitudes towards the essence.

* The essence is reflected in the form (one will adhere to the form because it complements and completes the essence).

Essence + form
Healing = being whole
God addresses the core/source
Restoration and relation
Choice (master or be mastered)

Your prayer:

DAY 27
three-in-one

«[The desert is…] a place where nobody desires by nature to be […] it is a place of purgation and temptation […] not to be lived in but to be entered into and crossed and travelled through. It is a place where meetings occur, and identities are lost and discovered in a silence that speaks […]»[103]

You have come across the story of the Israelites in the wilderness a few times in the days leading up to today. Think of today as this: instead of eating one delicious main course, you will be served with three scrumptious starters, each consisting of different ingredients, though their flavour profiles will be subtly linked.

Each of today's three passages is part of the larger narrative of the Israelites in the wilderness and reflects on a different aspect of their experience. Considering there are three exercises you will engage in today, I will keep the introduction brief and let you dive right in. You will notice that each passage is accompanied by a mini exercise, so as usual, complete one before reading on and completing the others, working sequentially and immersing yourself in each of the exercises…

a. Looking back, God provides

«Your clothes did not wear out upon you and your sandal did not wear out upon your foot.» Deuteronomy 29:4b

In this passage God is reminding them that even in their harshest, most trying times, He took care of them in every possible way.

Even though your journey takes you into the wilderness, a place where there is no one, God leads you, carries you, He watches you grow, and you prosper. The little that you possess does not fall apart, what covers you (clothes)

---
[103] David Jasper, *The Sacred Desert: Religion, Literature, Art and Culture*, (Oxford: Blackwell Publishing, 2004), 2.

and supports you (shoes) does not get worn out during your journey. God gives endurance to elements you need on your journey. He takes care of you, even in the seeming details.

Imagine yourself as a pair of shoes (or another item of clothing) of a person who is traveling through the wilderness... Write about your experience from your point of view of that item... Let your mind wander and be as descriptive as you wish... When you have finished your piece of writing, spend a few moments with it... What is its message...? Notice what those details (shoes, clothes) might be in your life that God has been providing and taking care of, despite what are at times difficult circumstances for you...

b. Cultivating the revealed

«The hidden things belong to YHVH our God but the things revealed belong to us and to our children forever to do all the words of this teaching.» Deuteronomy 29:28

A little later in chapter 29 comes this message concerning the hidden and revealed. Its essence is this:

There are things we don't know, things hidden from us that only God knows. But there are things that we can know, that have been made 'nude' [104] *for us, things we can discover. Like people in exile, out of their context, easily recognisable – these things are for us and for our children, forever. The reason they're accessible to us is so that we would do, make, create and accomplish them. These are things we can govern, provide for and with, things we can follow. These things belong to us, they are ours to know and to cultivate, forever.*

*We can expect to know the hidden things only once we cultivate what is already revealed.

---

[104] The Hebrew word *galah* (גָּלָה) means to *denude, reveal, uncover, to exile* (in the sense that captives were often stripped).

On a page in your notebook, draw a representation of the 'hidden' and the 'revealed' as it refers to your life... Once you have finished your drawings, consider each drawing and write down any words or thoughts that arise from each image (or both)... Note down ways in which you can put them into practice, live them. Why not decide to leave the 'hidden' to God while you focus on what has already been revealed to you?

c. Tailoring of the inner self

«*Then YHVH your God will open up your heart and the hearts of your offspring to love YHVH your God with all your heart and soul, that you may live.*» Deuteronomy 30:6

The word translated here as 'open up' is actually the word *mul* (מול) meaning *circumcision*, a word that might cause some of you to cringe. Here it encapsulates the idea of pruning, cutting some pieces away for the sake of well being in general (as one would an olive tree, for instance).[105]

God is the one who prepares your heart by cutting down unnecessary parts, pruning it, tailoring it, enabling you to completely love Him. He does this not only for you, but also for your children. When you allow God to do this, to have His way with the deepest, innermost parts of you, with your very soul, then you live, you are truly alive.

Even now as you are reading this, God is busy pruning you and you are increasingly becoming what He always envisioned you to be.

Imagine you are a tree that is being pruned, dead branches cut off, live branches cropped and shortened, leaves being removed as the shearing is in

---

[105] "In mature trees, pruning is mainly required to renew the fruiting surface of the tree and achieve high yields, maintain vegetative growth of fruiting shoots, maintain the skeleton structure, contain tree size, favour light penetration and air circulation inside the canopy, permit control of pests and diseases, prevent aging of the canopy, and eliminate dead wood. Under certain circumstances, pruning can be required to alleviate the effect of abiotic stress, to re-form the canopy after damage by frosts and pests, to rejuvenate old or abandoned trees [...]". http://www.oliveoilsource.com/page/olive-tree-pruning

process. Write a short passage about how you feel as the tree in this process, imagine it is an excerpt from the tree's journal you come across and read...

*   *   *

As a summary of today, notice which one of the three sections left the deepest impression on you, how it felt to do the exercises... In the usual manner, be attentive and listen to what it is saying... Write down any impressions or thoughts you may have...

Remember, God provides.
Cultivate what you know so far.
Pruning of the heart leads to life.
God longs to bless you.

Your prayer:

DAY 28

encouragement

«Indeed, YHVH your God has blessed you in all your undertakings. He knows your journey through this great wilderness; YHVH your God has been with you these past forty years: you have lacked nothing.» Deuteronomy 2:7

Many studies have identified a number of psychosocial factors that influence and predict our physical and mental health. Among them are stress, social support and social networks, competence, socio-economic status and coping.[106] The concept of social support is multifaceted and, without expanding on each aspect of it here, I will mention Dr Gerald Caplan who defined support systems as attachments between individuals and between individuals and groups that

1. validate identity by providing feedback about behaviour,
2. promote and help with the effective use of psychological resources in mastering the handling of emotional difficulties,
3. share in tasks and provide tangible and affective supplies.[107]

To know that we are watched over, that someone knows us, our journey, and that we are not alone even when we are experiencing our darkest hour – that has a powerful effect on the human psyche. Support in good times and especially in bad, leads us to believe that we are loved, cared for, valued and that we belong to a 'network of communication and mutual obligation.'[108]

On DAY 21 you read how God told the Israelites to face the road and prepare for their journey into the wilderness. They were told to pull their

---

[106] Barbara A. Israel, "Social Networks and Health Status: Linking theory, research and practice", *Patient Counselling and Health Education*, Vol. 4 (1982), 65-79.

[107] Gerald Caplan, M.D. *Support systems and community mental health: Lectures on Concept Development*, (Michigan: Behavioral Publications, 1974).

[108] Barbara A. Israel et al, "Social Networks among Elderly Women: Implications for Health Education Practice", *Health Education Quarterly*, Vol. 10 (1984), 173-203, quote on 175.

tent pins up and leave, but they did not. They delayed the journey into the wilderness by engaging in a battle God had warned them they would lose. After their defeat, they finally set out on their journey into the wilderness. Echoing yesterday's first text (Deuteronomy 29:4), today's passage is an invitation to reflect on God's goodness, an affirmation of His endless support.

Remember what God did for you in the past.

He blesses you; all your actions and transactions, whether good or bad, all the things you do or make with the strength and means you have available; God blesses and makes them turn out for the best. He sees you on your journey in the wilderness, He watches over you, He's aware of your every step, He understands the weight you carry, He knows you are growing (and prospering). He acknowledges your pursuit, your journey. Your journey is in a desert, a wilderness, a place where there is no one, only you and God, and He leads you, you listen to His voice, He is with you, and you lack nothing. There is not anything that you need that you do not have. You are not at a loss in any way (whether materially, experientially or otherwise) even though you are in the wilderness. God is with you throughout the whole journey, every minute, every day, every year, the whole time.

In the Western world it is a relatively standard practice to send out 'thank you' cards after one's wedding. It is a 'thank you' to your guests for having participated in such a joyous event with you, for their time and their gifts.

The occasion today is not a wedding but, in the quiet, allow yourself to remember what God has done for you in the past… Let your reflections not only encompass what He has *done*, but how and who He has *been*, how He has related with you… Let your mind move freely and follow where it leads… It could be quite far back… Without thinking too much, take a pen or pencil and your notebook and write a 'thank you' letter to God… This is your way of being aware of how you two have walked together in the past, and your way of thanking Him for whatever you feel you want to thank Him for… Let the pen write and do not think about the structure or wording, this is just between the two of you… Be honest and write whatever is in your heart… When you have finished, sit in silence for a few moments…

*   *   *

As you sit in silence, take your pen once more and begin to write

God's letter in response to you... This might seem daunting, but without allowing yourself to think, take your pen and begin...

*   *   *

How did it feel writing each letter?

Were you able to let it flow?

What did you remember, which memories surfaced?

What do you notice about those things that you have mentioned in your letter to God?

God's letter to you – what do you notice about it?

How would you describe the letter? Short, long, humorous, touching...?

In a few silent moments, consider both letters and their content...

Note down your impressions of what you wrote and what God wrote in return...

Write down how you feel in regard to both letters and what you might be learning or what insight you might be drawing from this exchange...

Reflect on encouragement and how much it means to you to feel supported and encouraged by God, those closest to you and even by those by which you did not expect to be encouraged...[109]

*   *   *

During their trudgings in the wilderness, I am sure it was a little more difficult for the Israelites to appreciate the extent to which God was taking care of them. It seems that when life becomes very difficult, almost intolerable, we are unable to notice all the details of our situation, blinded by our pain or other factors. But when the wave passes and the waters recede, the nuances of our past experiences begin to glisten and today's passage is an echo of that clarity in hindsight.

I first read this piece of writing below as a young child and it deeply impressed me. You may know it or you may not, but I share it with you

---

[109] We can only ever give what we ourselves have received. In the quiet, listen and notice if there are any individuals who you feel impressed to encourage today, in any way you find suitable... It could be a post-it, a letter, an email, a phone call, a visit... You may know them very well or it could be a complete stranger. Whoever it is, why not be a source of encouragement to someone else today?

as it helps put difficult situations in perspective and reminds me to look back and remember...

One night a man had a dream.

He dreamed he was walking along the beach with YHVH.

Across the sky flashed scenes from his life.

For each scene, he noticed two sets of footprints in the sand: one belonging to him, and the other to YHVH.

When the last scene of his life flashed before him, he looked back at the footprints in the sand. He noticed that many times along the path of his life there was only one set of footprints. He also noticed that it happened at the very lowest and saddest times in his life.

This really bothered him and he questioned YHVH about it.

"God, You said that once I decided to follow you, You'd walk with me all the way. But I have noticed that during the most troublesome times in my life, there is only one set of footprints. I don't understand why when I needed You most You would leave me."

YHVH replied, "My child, My precious child, I love you and I would never leave you. During your times of trial and suffering, when you see only one set of footprints, it was then that I carried you."

- Author Unknown

Journey ⇔ Growth
The journey is the better choice
All you need, you have
*Remember (He **knows**)*
The journey is blessed
God is with you

Your prayer:

DAY 29
a radical change

«If you thoroughly amend your ways and your actions; if you execute justice between one man and another; if you do not oppress the stranger, the orphan and the widow; and do not shed innocent blood in this place; if you do not follow other gods, to your own hurt – then only will I let you dwell in this place, in the land that I gave to your fathers for all time. See, you are relying on illusions that are of no avail.»
Jeremiah 7:5-8

Have you ever made a radical change of some kind? Perhaps it was chopping your hair off after a long relationship ended or taking up ice climbing as a hobby. When I think of radical changes, Dorian Paskowitz M.D. comes to mind. Dr Paskowitz was a Stanford graduate who one day closed down his successful medical practice to become a professional surfer. He and his Mexican-Indian wife led a bohemian life in a camper van with their nine children for many years. In the winters he would treat migratory workers, Native Americans and the urban needy; in the summers the whole family ran a surf camp for children in California. They would later become known as the 'First Family of Surfing.' Now that is what I call a radical change. Sometimes radical changes are something we stumble across in our old photo albums and wonder 'What was I thinking?!', yet at times some of our radical changes are gushes of fresh water into a stale swamp, profoundly altering our lives as they flow.

On DAY 19 you learnt about the *qal* Infinitive Absolute, one way in which crucial importance is stressed in the Hebrew language. It is that form that is used in the first sentence of today's passage: if you *really, really, thoroughly* amend your ways and doings... By using this form the author is immediately putting a literary magnifying glass on this part of the text, drawing our attention to what is to follow – it must be important.

Now that the author has captured your attention and got you really listening to him, keep listening as you read the paraphrase below based on the Hebrew text.

You really, really need to make the way you live your life at the moment better, you need to earnestly do what you think is best, to make a thorough change for the better. You really need to change your attitudes and how they play out in practice. When you make judgments about other people and situations, really, really do it with care and understanding; when you adhere to rules and regulations, do it with discernment and insight. Don't abuse or harm those who have no one to look out for them, who are marginalised, isolated from mainstream society; don't take your anger, frustration or whatever else out on people who have nothing to do with it. Don't follow other paths that are bad for you, that are wrong, harmful to you and cause you sorrow, trouble and misery; stop making choices that are not good for you. If you can and want to do this, you will be choosing truth over illusion. Then I will enable you to permanently settle down where I want you. It is not a physical location; it is near to My heart, when you closely relate to Me.

This is a call to make thorough changes, a call to sifting and shifting and not just on the surface, but deep within. There is also the reference to illusions; yet it is clothed in the garb of the marginalised – what do truth and illusion have to do with widows, orphans and the poor?

The notion of protecting these three groups of people is found in ancient literature from Mesopotamia to Israel. In antiquity kings and rulers considered it a virtue to take care of the marginalised. An early ancient Near Eastern example is the law of Babylonian King Hammurabi that stated that the strong were not to oppress the weak and that the widow and orphan should receive justice. However, whilst that may have been a law in antiquity, it was frequently not upheld and the orphans, widows and the poor often suffered greatly. Even today it is always the most vulnerable members of society that are affected most adversely.

«Widows, orphans and the poor were sold as credit-slaves and kept in a state of slavery for a lifetime [...] These people had no rights, no legal personalities, or in some cases restricted rights. They were almost outlaws. Anyone could oppress them without danger that legal connections might endanger his position.»[110]

---

[110] "A married woman had no legal personality after her husband's death, as was also the case with minor orphans. It was, thus, the duty of the king or monarch to

In 2004 psychologists Naomi Eisenberger and Matthew Lieberman conducted a study entitled 'Why Rejection Hurts' and found that the same area in the brain is activated in both social and physical pain.[111] In other words, whether you have an aching heart or an aching ear, for your brain it is much the same. It is no wonder then that we even have descriptive phrases for emotional pain such as 'a broken heart', 'heartache', 'homesick', etc. The duo also discovered that enhanced sensitivity to one type of pain (e.g. physical) enhances our sensitivity to another type of pain (e.g. emotional).

A few years later psychologist Kipling D. Williams revealed in his study that ostracism is 'the social kiss of death.'[112] People who are on the margins of society – for whatever reason in whatever capacity – feel invisible, unable to provoke any kind of response from others. They live in excruciating emotional pain and bearing in mind Eisenberger and Lieberman's study about the connection between types of pain, I would imagine that their outward circumstances only intensify their experience of pain.[113]

There is a saying that states something along the lines of: we are only as strong as our weakest link. Would you agree? Are we only as good as we are towards those who are alienated from the mainstream? In the context in which this passage arises, this seems to be the message coming through to the Israelites: you need to take a good look around you, how you treat those who are left by the way side; by ignoring them you are living in an illusion that

---

protect their rights in the same way as the father of the family should have done." F. Charles Fensham, "Widow, Orphan and the Poor in Ancient Near Eastern Legal and Wisdom Literature", *Journal of Near Eastern Studies*, Vol. 21 (1962), 129-139, quotes on 129, 132, 139.

[111] It is the right ventral prefrontal cortex. Naomi Eisenberger and Matthew Lieberman, "Why rejection hurts: a common neural alarm system for physical and social pain", *Trends in Cognitive Sciences*, Vol. 8 (7), 294-300.

[112] Williams watched as participants (while in an fMRI) played a game of Cyberball (throwing it back and forth) with who the participant believed were two other participants in the next room. When the other two players (whose icons were in fact controlled by the experimenter) stopped passing the ball to the observed participant, they felt rejected and hurt. This was accompanied by activation in the dorsal cingulated cortex. Kipling D. Williams, "Ostracism: the kiss of social death", *Social and Personality Psychological Compass* 1 (2007), 236-247.

[113] The last phase of ostracism, says Williams, is *self-ostracism*, in which the individual is caught in a vicious cycle of depression, often accompanied by suicidal thoughts, eating disorders, etc.

all is well.[114] Words are one thing, but whilst these people are still suffering your words mean nothing. You need to make a radical change, one that will stem from deep within your heart and be felt and seen in the way you are with others, especially with those who have no one to look out for them.

Quite a sobering message.
Radical change. Deep. Inward. Outward. Me. Others. Truth. Illusions.

*   *   *

Draw two outlines of your body shape (or trace the one in this book into your notebook), draw them as large as you can because of what follows (e.g. maybe on a bigger piece of paper that you will later staple in your notebook). Once you have, colour in one of the body shapes... Only read on when you have finished colouring that one in...

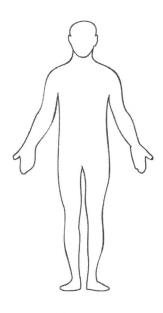

*   *   *

---

[114] The Hebrew word here is *sheqer* (שֶׁקֶר) meaning *deception, what deceives, disappoints and betrays one*. It can also be described as a 'sham'.

In your remaining body shape write anything (words/phrases/sentences, concrete or abstract) that is important to you, beneficial and helpful, things that you are choosing over those that hurt and harm you (you may choose to write them in different colours)... Do this without thinking, just let the words flow and they will find their way onto the paper...

*　　*　　*

Take a look at your body maps... What do you notice? What do you notice first?

How did it feel to fill each body map?

How did the experience of doing each one compare with the other?

Looking at your colour map, what do you notice about how you used the colours?

Is there one dominant colour or would you say it is equally colourful?

Did you use many colours or just a few or perhaps only one?

Do certain colours fill certain regions of the body?

Did you press lighter or harder with some colours or in some areas?

Looking at the body, which part of the body attracts your attention? Why?

Do the colours you have used remind you of anything?

Are there any common threads between this drawing and your previous drawings from days past? If so, explore the connection...

Looking now at the body map with words/phrases...

Are there any words (or word) that seem to stand out from the rest?

How do you feel about what you have written?

Notice which words fill which space in the body...

Do you perhaps feel a connection between where those words are on your body map and how you feel them in your body in your everyday experience?

Are there some words that are easier to 'live' than others?

Are there any patterns you notice about what you have written, any words that appear here that have cropped up in days past? If so, explore the connection...

Note down these and any other observations you make during your exploration...

*　　*　　*

On DAY 23 we considered how important it is to embody the principle and live the essence. Then, adding onto that, DAY 26 pointed out that the essence is connected with the form; how we are inside needs to correspond to the outside. Today's message is simply amplifying that connection and advocating an inward change of which the ripples are felt in the outside world.

Talking about radical changes is all well and good, but as we know, amending our ways is by no means an easy thing to do, at least it often seems that way. But perhaps we have more say in it than we might think or feel we do.

There are many ways to cross a field of tall grass, but if you consistently keep crossing it at one particular point, a path begins to form and each new time you come to that field it is easier to cross the field there without even giving it a second thought.

In the same way, we create pathways in our brain with our thoughts (known as the engagement of neuronal circuitry). By engaging in certain thought patterns we are technically firing the same group of neurons and that becomes a habit, both neuronally and behaviourally. Each neuron connects to an average of 10,000 other neurons and there are about 100 billion neurons all together.[115] As the number of neurons increases, the number of possible connections grows exponentially (e.g. for 2 neurons there are 2 possibilities for how they can be connected, for 3 neurons 8 possibilities, for 4 - 64, for 5 - 1,024, for 6 neurons 32,768, etc.).[116] Psychologist Donald Hebb explained it by simply saying *'Cells that fire together, wire together'*,[117] while Dr Jill Bolte Taylor phrases it this way:

«If I am not persistent with my desire to think about other things, and consciously initiate new circuits of thought, then those uninvited loops can generate new strength and begin monopolizing my mind again [...]

---

[115] Daniel J. Siegel, "Toward an Interpersonal Neurobiology of the Developing Mind: Attachment Relationships, 'Mindsight' and Neural Integration", *Infant Mental Health Journal*, Vol. 22 (2001), 67–94.

[116] Daniel J. Levitin, *This is Your Brain on Music*, (London: Atlantic Books, 2008), 87-88.

[117] Donald O. Hebb (1904-1985) was a Canadian psychologist who contributed to the fields of psychology and neuroscience most notably in what is known as Hebb's postulate (1949) summarised in the sentence mentioned above.

This does not mean I am in complete control of everything that happens to me. However, I am in control of how I choose to think and feel about those things.»[118]

In terms of our right and left hemisphere, as she puts it, the good news is that we

«[...] always have an alternative way of looking at any situation [...] If you approach me with anger and frustration, then I make the choice to either reflect your anger and engage in argument (left brain), or be empathic and approach you with a compassionate heart (right brain). What most of us don't realize is that we are unconsciously making choices about how we respond all the time.»[119]

The beauty of our potential to facilitate positive, radical changes that will sprout within us and then grow beyond, is that the more aware we are of what goes on within us, the more actively we can participate in our life on multiple levels. Whatever the radical, positive change be that we may seek, balance is paramount.

«Finding the balance between *observing* our circuitry and *engaging* with our circuitry is essential for our *healing*.»[120] (original emphasis)

It is extremely important for our overall health to understand that we have a **choice** about what goes on within. What Dr Bolte Taylor refers to here is being aware of habitual thought patterns and whether or not you choose to engage them, dive in and swim in them, over and over again. The alternative to letting your thoughts go on 'autopilot' is to observe the pull, the desire to hook into habitual circuits, acknowledge the emotions that arise in the given situation (not pretend they do not exist), and then consciously choose to think different thoughts. Imagine walking by a

---

[118] Bolte Taylor, *My Stroke of Insight*, 150, 153. She also adds "[…] it is vital to our health that we pay very close attention to how much time we spend hooked into the circuitry of anger, or the depths of despair." This can have "devastating consequences on our physical and mental well being because of the power they have over our emotional and physiological circuitry." 155.
[119] Bolte Taylor, *My Stroke of Insight*, 147.
[120] Bolte Taylor, *My Stroke of Insight*, 154.

bakery and you feel the almost irresistible urge to go inside and feast on all the donuts they have on display. Rather than hurriedly walking by and facing the other direction, one hand up to block your view of the shop window, you face the window head on, acknowledge the desire, then choose to keep on walking. In more Freudian terms, this would mean that we acknowledge and process rather than deny or repress psychic material.

Be courageous and make thorough, beneficial changes in your life; then curiously observe what happens as a result…

Your prayer:

DAY 30
truth & illusion

Before we dive into today's story, stop for a moment and imagine this: you have two friends – one prefers routines, likes to eat at her favourite restaurant ordering her favourite meal, always wears a seat belt and writes conscientious book reviews on Amazon. The other friend of yours is a little on the wild, some would say reckless, side. He occasionally sticks gum under tables, likes to eat at a new place each time you meet, travels light and in unknown directions and does not write book reviews (or any other reviews) for that matter.

You have quit your job and you are at the point in your life where something really needs to change. After some deliberation it is done – you decide to buy a one-way ticket to Peru. Which friend will you go to for advice? Now press «PAUSE» and hold that thought as you read on.

«There was a lull of three years, with no war between Aram and Israel.»[121]

One day King Jehoshaphat of Judah comes to visit Ahab, the King of Israel.[122] The King of Israel says to his courtiers,

«'You know that Ramoth-gilead [123] *belongs to us, and yet we do nothing to recover it from the hands of the king of Aram.'»*

---

[121] The Arameans were a western Semitic people. After the division of the Israelite kingdoms Aram became the strongest of the small states of the region, dominating Upper Mesopotamia. From the time of Ahab (1 Kgs 20, 22) Israel and Aram were regularly at war, until Jeroboam II regained a dominant position.

[122] Ahab (King of northern Israel) was the son and successor of Omri, the founder of Samaria. Inheriting his father's military virtues he successfully defended his kingdom from the Syrian kingdom of Damascus. He married Jezebel, daughter of Ethbaal, King of Tyre, and with that family alliance he cemented his relationship with the Phoenicians. While that alliance was politically and commercially beneficial for Israel, it brought moral and spiritual ruin (1 Kgs 16:30-32). http://www.jewishencyclopedia.com

[123] Also known as Ramoth in Gilead – it was one of the safe cities (see DAY 18) east of the Jordan River, belonging to the tribe of Gad (Deut. 4:43, Josh. 20:8; 21:38).

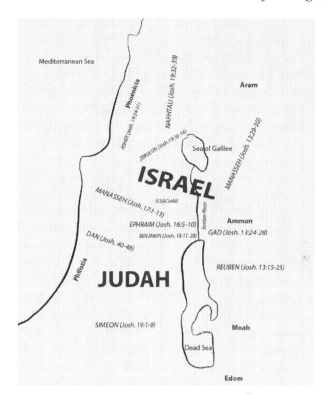

So he asks Jehoshaphat:

«Will you come with me to battle at Ramoth-gilead?»

Jehoshaphat answers the King of Israel and says,

«I will do what you do; my troops shall be your troops, my horses shall be your horses.»

But Jehoshaphat adds, under one condition:

«Please, first inquire of YHVH.»

So the King of Israel agrees and gathers the prophets, about four hundred men, and asks them,

«Shall I march upon Ramoth-gilead for battle, or shall I not? 'March', they say, *'and YHVH will deliver [it] into Your Majesty's hands.'»*

But Jehoshaphat notices something is odd so he asks Ahab if there is someone missing,

«Isn't there another prophet of YHVH here through whom we can inquire?"

And the King of Israel answers Jehoshaphat and admits that

Today the precise location of Ramoth-gilead is unknown.

«*There is one more man through whom we can inquire of YHVH; but I hate him, because he never prophesies anything good for me, but only misfortune – Micaiah son of Imlah.*»

King Jehoshaphat pauses for a moment and then says, «*Don't say that, Your Majesty.*» So the King of Israel decides to call that prophet, he summons an officer and says, «*Bring Micaiah son of Imlah.*»

Arrayed in their robes the King of Israel and King Jehoshaphat of Judah are seated on their thrones, on the threshing floor at the entrance of the gate of Samaria, and all the prophets are prophesying before them. All the prophets are prophesying good fortune and victory in battle. One after the other they come and are all saying the same thing.

Now, the messenger that the King of Israel has sent to get the prophet Micaiah notices that all the other prophets are predicting victory, so as he is bringing Micaiah to the King, he suggests to Micaiah:

«*[...] let your word be like that of the rest of them; speak a favourable word.*»

But Micaiah responds:

«*As YHVH lives, I will speak only what YHVH tells me.*»

So they arrive before the King of Israel and he asks Micaiah

«*Micaiah, shall we march upon Ramoth-gilead for battle or shall we not?*»

Micaiah says

«*March and triumph! YHVH will deliver [it] into Your Majesty's hands.*»

A little unnerved, the king says to him

«*How many times must I adjure you to tell me nothing but the truth[124] in the name of YHVH?*»» In other words, I know you are saying what I want to hear, just tell me the truth, go on. So Micaiah then tells him that he sees

«*Israel scattered all over the hills like sheep without a shepherd [...]*»

otherwise said: don't go, it won't end well.

The King of Israel turns to King Jehoshaphat and remarks with an 'I

---

[124] Just a reminder of DAY 3 and the meaning of 'truth' in the ancient Israelite context: "Indeed the Hebrew understanding of truth is expressed by means of words stemming from the verb '*aman*' – to be steady, faithful; constancy, faithfulness, trustworthiness, fidelity to reported facts. The Hebrews really do not ask what is true in the objective sense but what is subjectively certain, what is faithful in the existential sense." Boman, *Hebrew Thought Compared with Greek*, 202.

told you so': «*Didn't I tell you that he would not prophesy good fortune for me but only misfortune?*»

After a few more twists and turns in the story the King of Israel has Micaiah sent to prison and as he is being taken away Micaiah says to the King: «*If you ever come home safe, YHVH has not spoken through me.*» 1 Kings 22:1-18

Before we find out what happened in the end, we will press «PLAY» and continue on with you and your two friends: whom do you go to for advice? Knowing the one is adventurous and inclined to escapades of such a sort as you have up your sleeve, you know he will encourage you and cheer you on. On the other hand, if you talk to your other friend about it, she will probably be more apprehensive, possibly reciting a long list of potential hazards along the way. If you are really intent on going then she will just be 'raining on your parade'.

The King of Israel seems quite intent on going into battle and he has a decision to make. After conferring with King Jehoshaphat he decides to honour his request to ask God for advice. Seemingly he does just that, he calls all the four hundred prophets in the city purposely leaving out Micaiah, the one who has a tendency of 'raining on his parade'. Yet, as the situation unfolds and he hears what he does not want to hear, what do you think happens? Do they march into battle or not? They decide to march after all and – it ends badly as Micaiah warned. The misfortune of the King of Israel finds him indeed and he dies.[125]

You first encountered the theme of illusions in the context of optical illusions on DAY 13. It accentuated the notion that although all our options might seem the same, equally good or valuable, how are we to know if it is really so? Today's text deepens that rift and the difference between truth and illusion is no small matter in today's story. It is quite literally a matter of life or death.

Just imagine the scene – four hundred or so prophets who are saying "March!" and one who is saying "Don't.". As Micaiah said, if you come home safe today then God did not speak through me and what I said was not the truth. It could not have been both ways, the King would either return safely or he would not; either the four hundred prophets were telling the truth or Micaiah was – it remained to be seen.

---

[125] Ironically, he had even disguised himself as a commoner to avoid being killed.

Belinda É. Samari

Before we move on, consider these few notions from today's story... Notice if any one of them speaks to you in particular...

- o *Sometimes we try and defy God's word and will for our lives by going in exactly the opposite direction*
- o *God's word always prevails*
- o *We try to tailor God's word to suit us*
- o *Consult God before making major plans and decisions*
- o *Illusions have well-crafted, near-to-perfect masks resembling truth*

Moving on now let me ask you, are you familiar with the Russian Matryoshka dolls, the ones that are nested one inside the other? The first dolls are believed to have been based on an old Japanese tradition and were created in Russia at the end of the 19th century.[126] Each doll is cut in half and can be opened; when it is, it reveals a smaller doll inside it and that doll, when opened, reveals an even smaller doll inside itself. The bigger the first doll, the more little ones it can embody. Though one can anticipate it, one never knows exactly what the next doll will be like or how small the last doll will be. Though the rosy-cheeked woman in a bold headscarf is the most common type of Matryoshka doll, the most expensive versions of the dolls depict scenes from Russian fairy tales, each doll opening up to reveal the next part of the story. Much like truth and illusion, though the doll may look one way on the outside, we can never know what it contains within. Here is an example of the dolls:

---

[126] http://legomenon.com/russian-matryoshka-nesting-dolls-meaning.html

As usual, find a quiet place where you will be undisturbed... Have your notebook and (colouring) pencils and/or other tools prepared... While you are noticing your inner chatter, allow each thought, each distracting sentence in your mind to leave... When you have cleared your creative space and are ready, bearing in mind the theme of truth and illusion, imagine a set of unpainted Matryoshka dolls and draw them into your notebook. Draw as many dolls as you like; you may want to draw one at a time or draw them all at once and then proceed to fill them – follow your intuition... Letting it flow, begin to fill in the biggest one in any way you wish, (begin with that one as that is the only one that is first seen, the rest of them are hidden one inside the other). Fill in each one as you go along...

*   *   *

Looking at your dolls, what do you notice?
Are they colourful or 'black and white' (just pencil)?
At first glance, does your drawing remind you of something? If so, of what?

If the dolls are more like 'people', imagine you are meeting the dolls for the first time and would like to know more about them... Ask them questions... You might want to start by asking questions that refer to them more generally (as a group perhaps) and then move onto more specific questions regarding each doll in particular... Here are a few to get you started...

How many 'dolls' are there (does that number mean anything to you)?

What are they like, how would you describe them?

Are they part of a whole or do they seem very different from each other?

What are their personalities like?

Where do they come from?

Do they have names?

Do they have any particular characteristics?

Ask each doll how it feels to be inside the other... ask each doll how it feels to contain another doll within itself...

If the dolls perhaps depict an unfolding story, then notice what the theme of the story is... If the story had a name, what would it be?

Who are the main characters?

What happens?

What does each scene/doll look like?

Do you have any favourites?

Any you particularly dislike?

Be free with your questions and notice anything your drawing might be telling you... The content is already there, all you need to do is listen and observe... Note down your impressions and thoughts...

*   *   *

How are the threads of truth and illusion woven into your drawing? Did you feel them quite consciously in your mind as you were immersed in the creative process, or are you more aware of them now as you reflect on your artwork?

Truth and *illusion* is what it all boils down to – the difference between truth and illusion in your life, in this world, in the entire universe. What is and what masquerades as what is, reality and our projected reality. The two inevitably part as they cannot hold together very long. Truth or illusion, it cannot be both.

Reflect on these two concepts... How can you practically identify them in your life?

Do you feel as though you are aware of them or does the line separating them seem blurred? Can you perhaps feel them intuitively but are not able to articulate what the truth and illusion(s) might be? If so, what might you and God together be able to do to make the distinction clearer?

If the distinction is clear to you, do you find yourself – for one fear or another – still clutching illusions? How could that change? What would you ask from God to do from His side? What could you do from yours?

Your prayer:

DAY 31
perfect

Today we are jumping off the board and plunging straight in! Without turning the book upside down or trying too hard to decipher it, take a leisurely stroll through the text below and circle (or note down) words that catch your eye...

how He wants it to be: complete, truth, whole.
a full life. He sets me free and enables my way of life, my path, to be precisely
me down, things that are holding me back, things that prevent me from living
should have bound me to begin with. He releases me from things that weigh
every sense of the word. God sets me free. He unties me from things that never
integrity, to be complete, sincere, undefiled, whole. That path is 'entire' in
God's path for me, the way He wants me to live my life, is in truth,

          *   *   *

Now that you have noted down what you picked up along your stroll, read today's passage.

«*The way of God is perfect, the word of YHVH is pure. He is a shield to all who take refuge in Him […] God is my strength and power: and He makes my way perfect.*»
2 Samuel 22:31,33

The Oxford dictionary defines 'perfect' as: 'having all the required or desirable elements, qualities, or characteristics; as good as it is possible to be.'[127] When we hear 'perfect' most of us think 'faultless' and 'flawless', yet we still think of the perfect house, the perfect wedding, the perfect partner, the perfect vacation, the perfect job, the perfect retirement. It seems we are always striving for some sort of 'perfection'. What we may not be aware

---

[127] http://www.oxforddictionaries.com/definition/english/perfect

of is that the way we understand perfection greatly impacts our choices, including how we live our lives and how we treat others and also ourselves.

Today's passage says: God's way is perfect… He makes my way perfect. But what does that *perfect* mean? Does it mean that my life's path will be faultless and flawless? If that is the case then I am out of the game and heading for the benches.

The word 'perfect' here is *tamiym* (תָּמִים), meaning 'complete, whole, entire' (literally/figuratively/morally) derived from *tamam* (תָּמַם) meaning to 'be complete, finished.' In today's context it refers to God's way as 'sound, wholesome, unimpaired, innocent, having integrity.'[128]

Just as the word 'healing' stemmed from the root of wholeness and completeness (DAY 23), so today's word 'perfect' means first and foremost to be complete as a person, to have integrity and be wholesome in the fullest sense.

If you will, walk your way through today's paraphrase based on the Hebrew text (this time the right way up!) and let the words fall on you, feel their weight… (notice which words you circled/wrote down after your first upside-down reading)…

God's path for me, the way He wants me to live my life, is in truth, integrity, to be complete, sincere, undefiled, whole. That path is 'entire' in every sense of the word. God sets me free, He unties me from things that never should have bound me to begin with, He releases me from things that weigh me down, things that are holding me back, things that prevent me from living a full life. He sets me free and enables my way of life, my path, to be precisely how He wants it to be: complete, truth, whole.

The notion of God's way being perfect and also making our way perfect, shows that we are somehow able to know what that way is, and also trust that it is perfect. Until now we have considered truth and illusion in regard to our choices (DAY 22) and also the experience of being at a crossroads, waiting and wanting to know which path is best (DAY 24).

---

[128] Francis Brown D.D., D.Litt., *A Hebrew and English Lexicon of the Old Testament based on the lexicon of William Gesenius as translated by Edward Robinson*, (Boston and New York: Houghton Mifflin Co., The Riverside Press Cambridge), 1071. Also available online https://archive.org/stream/hebrewenglishlex00geseuoft#page/n5/mode/2up

There is an element of revelation that keeps weaving its way through our journey. The question is, how are we to know God's way, that perfect and best way for us? How can we know that we are on the right path?

When we are infants how do we 'know' the world around us? Our knowledge is an implicit knowing (not cognitive function *per se*) that consists of the physiological, social and behavioural regulation that is carried out between our caregiver and us as infants. We 'remember' the way in which our caregiver interacted with us and this becomes the blueprint of our understanding of relationships, of how the world functions and our place in it. This knowledge is based on our history of how to be with another, and that is based on emotion, sensations and action, not on words and symbols.[129]

«God revealed himself to the Israelites in history and not in Ideas; He revealed Himself when He acted and created. His being was not learned through propositions but known in actions.»[130]

Much like we come to know our parents or caregivers through our daily interactions with them over prolonged periods of time, so history has been God's way of revealing Himself to us. We come to know Him based on how He relates to us and what He does.

Our lives are a story and phrases such as 'I've lost the plot' or 'They have a history' testify to this fact as we continuously use them in our everyday language. Not only is history the way in which God has been making Himself known and available to us until now, but history can also be understood as

---

[129] This implicit knowledge is not more primitive though it is not language-based. It is not replaced by the appearance of language nor transformed into language later in development. In other words, we retain this intuitive knowing of the world throughout our lives. Boston Change Process Study Group, "The Foundational Level of Psychodynamic Meaning: Implicit Processes in Relation to Conflict, Defense and the Dynamic Unconscious", *International Journal of Psychoanalysis*, 88 (2007), 843-860.

[130] Boman, *Hebrew Thought Compared with Greek,* 171. In other words, God revealed Himself to the Israelites not in the propositional knowing characteristic of the LH, but in the experience of the RH that unfolded over time (of which 'history' is the culmination).

«[...] a movement toward a goal which is set by God.»[131]

If that is true of the history of humankind as a whole, then could it be that the same is true of our lives, of our 'little histories' that fit into the larger one?

Could it be that God is uniquely revealing Himself to us in our life stories?

If we accept that notion to be true then our lives, too, are 'a movement toward a goal which is set by God'. Our lives have a purpose and all of the events therein are interrelated, weaving a story larger than the sum of its seeming fragments.

For today's creative process you will need your notebook and something with which to draw. Find a quiet place where you will be free to immerse yourself in the creative flow... As usual, slowly quiet your LH chatter and be still... Before starting, read till the end of the paragraph and then begin... You will take a pencil in your hand (coloured or not) and draw a line, any kind of line, curved or straight, long or short... What you will be doing is drawing something (it is yet to reveal itself to you) stroke by stroke... The key is to put all thoughts aside and draw one line at a time, following your intuition... As you draw each line, be aware of it and feel it as it sinks into the page... Slowly as you go along, your drawing will be forming, line by line, move by move... Do not worry or think about what it will become, whether geometrical or a portrait, a shape of this kind or that... Simply place a line on a paper one at a time and take your time with it (with the whole process and also between lines)... *Do not erase or scribble out any line you draw*... If for some reason it does not feel right, just keep going and stay in the flow... Keep drawing only as long as it flows, notice when 'the lines run out' and the last one has been put on the paper.

Begin when you are ready...

*　　　*　　　*

How did this process feel?

Were you in the creative flow or did you find you were thinking about what you were doing (if you were thinking, what were you thinking about and what might be the cause for your distraction)?

---

[131] Boman, *Hebrew Thought Compared with Greek*, 171.

How would you describe the process of slowly giving birth to a drawing one line at a time?

How did it feel to not know what would finally appear on the paper?

Looking at your artwork, how would you describe what you have drawn?

Is it in colour or not?

Is it something you recognise or perhaps cannot quite define?

Note down your description of it, feel free to be elaborate...

Notice any associations or memories that might surface...

The *process* of creation is always more important than the end product, and so it is in this case. We are contemplating perfection today and the idea that our life is made perfect (whole and complete) as it continually unfolds, line by line, day by day. Much like the process you just engaged in, we do not know the outcome of our days in advance.

With that in mind, reflect on today's creative process (how it felt and what came of it - your drawing) and the concept of perfection as completion, as something that is on-going and moving along with a purpose...

*   *   *

We hear 'perfection' and we think it means being without flaws, no mistakes allowed. But that is not at all what it means. As you learnt on DAY 23 your attitude plays an immensely important role in your journey. If you are open and listening with your heart set on Him, God will make you (and the rest of the components in your life) complete, sound, whole. You will live your life in truth and with integrity.

If you look back over your life up until this point it is highly likely that you will begin to trace God in your life, one line at a time. Begin to notice patterns and themes that speak to you about Him and how He relates to you personally... Explore this and note down your observations...

Your prayer:

the field

«Sow righteousness for yourselves, reap the fruit of unfailing love (chesed), and break up your unploughed ground; for it is time to seek YHVH, until He comes and rains His righteousness on you.» Hosea 10:12

Have you ever done a hard day's work outside, filling your lungs with fresh air, hands dug deep into the soil, dirt under your fingernails, sweat on your brow? Most of us live in urban spaces where the nearest shrub is in our neighbourhood park and digging up the soil would be unseemly. Many of us have rarely spent time in the countryside let alone worked on a field, but for those of you who have and perhaps still do, I imagine you will especially enjoy today's topic.

Read through today's passage and notice the verbs: sow... reap... break up (plough)... These things all speak about the process of agriculture, 'the science, art and practice of cultivating the soil...'.[132] There is a way to handle the earth, and there is a process that creates the right kind of environment in which growth is enabled and nurtured. These verbs in today's passage are followed by '*seek* YHVH until He comes and *rains* His righteousness on you'. But before we get to the rain, let us look at what precedes it.

Before sowing, reaping, or the rain, comes ploughing. Ploughing the soil (also known as tilling, and I prefer that word for no special reason) is an important part of processing the earth. During the long winter months when the soil is untouched, it hardens and becomes quite stiff. When the land is undisturbed and solid, planting anything in it is very difficult without tilling it first. To till the soil means to turn it over, to break it up and soften it as today's text says.

The most common time to till soil is before planting season, which makes sense. Tilling loosens up the soil, it gives the plants room to expand and kills weeds and other plants that would compete for nutrients. But before the tilling begins the ground must be dry enough and warm enough.

---

[132] http://www.merriam-webster.com/dictionary/agriculture

If one does not wait for these two conditions then more harm than good will be done. Once the tilling has begun it should not be rushed and each row should be tilled only once.[133]

Now consider the element of rain in this process. «When rain falls on the surface of a tilled soil, it may be that exposed surfaces [...] are able to absorb the rain.»[134] Tilling not only loosens the soil thereby providing more oxygen and space for growth, it also allows the earth to soak in the raindrops, which is a crucial element in the growth process.

Of the actions mentioned above all bar one are down to you and me – they are in our hands, so to speak. We can sow, reap, plough and even seek God, but the rain, that we have no control over. That belongs to God and His timing; for that we can ask and then wait until we feel the pitter-patter...

Get comfortable wherever you are...[135] As usual, ensure you will have peace and quiet and will not be disturbed. Before you do the exercise, have your pencils and paper/notebook nearby as you will need them later on. When you are ready, gently close your eyes... quiet your inner chatter and notice as it fades... Focus on your breathing and be aware of your body.

(Before you dive into your imagination, whilst you are there, take note of anything and everything that is brought to your attention...)

Imagine a field... See it in your imagination...

Have a good look around you...

Notice how you feel being there... Feel the earth beneath your feet...

Take a breath, what can you smell...?

Turning your attention to the sounds, what can you hear...?

Spend as much time in that field as you feel you want to...

When you have spent sufficient time there, slowly bring your attention back to the place where you are and gently open your eyes...

---

[133] A. R. Dexter, "Physical properties of tilled soils", *Soil and Tillage Research* Vol. 43 (1997), 41-63.

[134] Dexter, Physical properties, 48.

[135] If you are surrounded by fields in your area, you might want to go and lie down in the middle of a field and do this exercise, feeling the earth beneath you, putting yourself in a different space to reflect and experience...

Without any hesitation, take your pencils and paper and depict what you saw in your imagination...

*   *   *

How did it feel to be in the field (internally/externally)?

What were you focusing on while you were in the field?

How would you describe your field?

How is the soil?

Do you know where the field is located (near a road, way out in the middle of nowhere)?

Do you tend it and work on it, or do others, or no one?

Is there anything growing on it? If so, what?

Is it tidy and neat or more on the wild side?

Are you alone or is there someone with you?

What are you doing there? Is this your first time there or is that place familiar?

What are the main elements of the image in your mind?

If your field could speak, what would it say to you? It might be a word or another image that appears... What does its message mean to you? What are the implications of its message? If you are not sure right away what it might mean, sit with it for a while, let it speak... Notice any associations or memories that might arise... If you are not sure even after giving yourself the space to explore, come back to it another time, engage it in the way that feels best and take it from there...

*   *   *

In your field, your life, plant what is truthful, sow what is right. Reap whatever grows in your field and as you cut it down, give yourself time to mourn, to grieve, knowing that you are doing a good deed; you will feel God's unfailing love and His mercy as you do. Break up the soil of your life, revive it, take care of it; it's hard work but you have to do it for it to be good in the long run. If you do, your life will be brighter, glowing and gleaming, refreshed. Deal with your life – it can get neglected unless you attend to it; you might have wanted to delay the breaking up of the ground in your field, to leave it for

179

the next season, but this is the time, you must do it now. Seek God, search for Him, ask Him, do it over and over again, consult Him, seek Him out. He's in a personal, covenantal relationship with you, He exists, He won't leave you or ignore you. Keep searching, asking, inquiring until He comes and stays with you, until He makes some things happen, until He points out the way, until He teaches you what you need to know (at that moment), until He directs you, instructs you, informs you, shows you. Until He does this like pouring rain, refreshing you, obvious and abundant, and this rain will be what is right, it will be according to His standard; it will be right in every possible way.

Today's passage is a call to action: go, do, sow, reap, break up the ground, seek God and keep doing so until the rain comes! Before you is the challenge to break up the soil, to do the necessary preparatory work so that you can plant good things in your field and enjoy the wonderful results. The ploughing, sowing and harvesting is for you to do, that is your part and your privilege. It endows you with a sense of ownership and participation in your present and future. This is a message of encouragement for you to do what lies within your hands until God comes and rains on the field, on you and your life, so that what you have sown will begin to bud and grow...

Your prayer:

DAY 33
the big picture

«For I am mindful of the plans I have made concerning you – declares YHVH – plans for your welfare, not for disaster, to give you a hopeful future.» Jeremiah 29:11

Key characters: The Israelites.

The setting: The Neo-Babylonian Empire (mainly present day Iraq). Jehoiachin King of Judah has surrendered to King Nebuchadnezzar and been taken captive to Babylon along with some 10,000 of Jerusalem's principal citizens.[136]

Have you ever moved from one place to another, willingly or by way of necessity? Maybe you were a refugee at one time in your life and had to flee from your home, maybe you had to move to a foreign country or continent for work or maybe you have lived in the same place all your life. Regardless, take a moment now to imagine this uprooting and what it must have been like for them…

The exiled Judeans (as they were commonly called at the time) are now in a foreign land, surrounded by new people who speak a new language and they have to adjust to this foreign *milieu*. They have to adapt, readjust and redefine their identity and place in this new setting. In a sudden turn of events their lives have completely changed.

It is at this time that the prophet Jeremiah writes a letter (chapter 29 from verse 4 onwards) to the deported who are now in Babylon, a message from 'YHVH of Israel' to 'the whole community which I exiled from Jerusalem to Babylon'. It begins with the words:

«Build houses and live in them, plant gardens and eat their fruit.»

I'm sorry, do what? What did You say, build houses and plant gardens? Are You sure? We're in captivity!

---

[136] Recorded in 2 Kgs 24:12-15.

«Take wives and beget sons and daughters; and take wives for your sons and give your daughters to husbands, that they may bear sons and daughters. Multiply there, do not decrease.»

So just checking: not only are we supposed to build houses, but we're actually supposed to settle down? Here, really? Even have children and grandchildren? We were hoping this would be over before then...

«And seek the welfare of the city to which I have exiled you and pray to YHVH in its behalf; for in its prosperity you shall prosper.»

A little further on He tells them:

«When Babylon's seventy years are over, I will take note of you, and I will fulfil to you My promise of favour – to bring you back to this place.»

Then come the beautiful words of today's passage:

«For I am mindful of the plans I have made concerning you – declares YHVH – plans for your welfare, not for disaster, to give you a hopeful future.»

I can imagine that they might have been confused by the message as it was probably not what they had been expecting to hear. They had not been expecting this, God had not intervened to prevent their exile and here they were, captive in a foreign land. Questions abounded.

Yet though it may have been confusing, the message was clear. Lovingly God tells them: live your lives, plant gardens and eat the fruit they bear; seek peace in the city you are in and enjoy it. Have families, have many children and when they grow up, celebrate as they get married and go on to have families of their own. In other words, go about life as usual, adapt, even though your circumstances are unusual.

God promises them that after seventy years of Babylonian captivity, He will deliver them, He will enable them to return to Jerusalem, to their home. He also adds the words we find in today's text. Comforting them He says that even though they do not know what the future brings, He does, because He is above and beyond what they perceive and imagine. What

He has in mind for them is only for their good and not to harm them in any way (including where they are at that moment).

After this passage in verse 11 He continues to tell them: you will search for Me, seek Me out and I will be there for you, I will hear you. Now you are spread out, a scattered people, but it will not always be this way, I will gather you again.

«Disaster and sorrow compel either a soul or a nation to seek anew the foundations of life. Times of sorrow are accordingly times of religious growth. The Babylonian exile was no exception.»[137]

In the midst of our struggles, in our darkest periods when we feel exiled and abandoned, that is also the time when we are most likely to dig deeper, to search for food that truly nourishes the soul because all that is on the surface seems to fall away, exposed in all its insignificance. It is often in those times that we search our hearts and face some hard truths.

«[...] the effect of the fall of Jerusalem can hardly be overestimated. Since God did not appear to protect the city unconditionally, entirely new answers to old questions needed to be formulated, and a new relationship to the word of YHWH was needed – answers that are being sought in the book of Jeremiah [...] the crisis situation in itself would not have meant anything, had not a group of people been ready to search for a new significance of temple [...] covenant, and many other aspects of faith. Inside that movement, creative and renewing [...] work took place.»[138]

As difficult as the exile was for the Judeans, the questions they now had to face (and find answers to) they easily could have kept on ignoring had they stayed in their comfort zone. This is not to say the exile was unavoidable, not at all. But equally so it is often only when we are stretched beyond what feels to be our limit, that we grow dramatically and become people of more breadth and depth. It seems that God knew the potential

---

[137] George A. Barton, "Influence of the Babylonian Exile on the Religion of Israel", *The Biblical World,* Vol. 37 (6) 1911, 369-378.
[138] Joep Dubbink, "Getting Closer to Jeremiah: The word of YHWH and the Literary-Theological Person of a Prophet" in *Reading the Book of Jeremiah: A Search for Coherence*, Martin Kessler (ed.), (Winona Lake, IN: Eisenbrauns, 2004), 33.

these unusual albeit painful circumstances held in store for those who were willing to embrace the process and implications of this radical change.

«In the years of struggle [...] Jeremiah had under its shadow grasped the great truth that religion is inward in character, that it is a matter of the heart, and that no outward temple or ritual is necessary to its maintenance [...] God's covenant with His people was to be a covenant of the heart [...]»[139]

And note that God did not just leave them there. He gave them a promise to hold on to.

On DAY 25 we talked about time and the ancient Israelite perspective – the past is laid bare before us, while the future comes after us. In Hebrew the word *achar* (אחר) means 'back', 'behind', and of the time 'after'. From that word comes *acharit* (אַחֲרִית) which you encountered on DAY 25, meaning 'hindermost side, that which comes after'. It is *acharit* that is translated as 'future' in today's text. That phrase literally means to give you 'future and hope' (*acharit* and *tiqvah*, see DAY 8).

Today the message is the same for you as it was for the captive Judeans thousands of years ago: even though your circumstances might (still) be limiting, restricting, difficult, painful and out of your immediate control, you have the opportunity to go deeper and therefore, to grow. Make the most of where you are now, build your houses and plant your gardens and remember: though it may not seem that way, there are plans in place for your life and your unique story is slowly unfolding.[140]

I have chosen to leave today's creative exercise, which is also the last one in this book, without any pointers or guidance... By now you have significantly developed your RH, your abilities to visualise, intuitively and nonverbally express your inner being. I happily leave it to you and your inspiration drawn from today's text, to express your inner content in

---

[139] Barton, "Influence of the Babylonian Exile on the Religion of Israel", 370.

[140] After 70 years Jeremiah's words were fulfilled and the Judeans were free to return to Jerusalem (see 2 Chronicles 36:22-23; Ezra 1:1-4). Cyrus of Persia conquered Babylon and in the very first year of his reign he decreed that the Judeans could return to Jerusalem to rebuild their temple.

whichever way you wish... When you have done that, follow your intuition and notice what surfaces and make note of it, as you have done until now...

*　　　*　　　*

(Your name) _____*, I am very well aware of the plans I have for you. I understand them, I know them and am sure of them. I recognise you, I care for you, I watch you and I know what I want for you in the future. I am diligent when it comes to the purpose of your life. I weave these plans, I devise them for you, give them meaning and a purpose. These intentions of Mine for your life are for you to be whole, safe, happy; to be at peace with yourself and others, to find true rest, for all to be well in every aspect of your life. In My plans for you, there is not a trace of anything that will hurt you or harm you; these plans are not ethically wrong, they won't make you miserable, sorrowful, they won't get you into trouble, won't make you unhappy. They won't make things worse than they are now, they won't be displeasing to you or cause you distress. What I want to give you, without fail, is a connection, a hope – at the end of this phase of your journey and also in general in your life. I want to restore you and heal you, now and in the long-term. I want to give you the outcome you long for (and I will).*

Hold onto this promise and never let it go.

*　　　*　　　*

IN CLOSING

Dear Reader,

You have come a long way... Looking back, you can trace your growth through the things you have written, drawn, and experienced, and you are certainly further along your path now than when you first began this journey. Perhaps you have already experienced some significant unfolding and have received answers for which you were searching. Perhaps you have partial answers or a collection of fragments whilst the big picture still remains obscured. Whatever it may be, this is not the end... You are on your path, on His path for you and God has sustained you and brought you this far. He will not leave you now, of this you can be sure.

In the past 33 days (or so) you have awakened your right hemisphere and have invited both left and right to communicate and create together. You have opened yourself to another dimension of processing information, of reasoning, of expressing who you are and the nuances of what you think and feel.[141] I hope that you will continue with creative endeavours like this – if not every day, often. When you do, instead of reading and doing what is assigned, be open to the unknown. Dare to venture into unchartered territory and see where God will lead you in and by His word. Allow yourself to be creative. Each of us has our own story to tell that stems from our unique connection with God. What happens on the pages from now onwards is up to you, it is your story, your unique experience documented in a way that will be a treasure to you, and most likely to others in the future.

---

[141] Our inner images are like mirrors, ways in which we can monitor and be aware of our internal movements. As we are fluid, so are they and they change over time. You can revisit your drawings in a few months or years, and be able to notice how they have changed, how they have been transformed, etc. You can also engage this book all over again in a year or five years from now and your drawings will not be the same – the mirrors will be the same but what you will see in them will be entirely different, reflecting your inner self at that very moment in time. In other words, these creative exercises are not only a template to help launch you into the creative world of the right and left hemisphere, but will always contain the potential to be effective, stirring and inspiring.

I hope you have been encouraged, strengthened and emboldened to continue and not give up when you grow weary, even though it will get difficult at times. Growth rarely occurs when life is easy (if at all). With an earnest heart and the willpower to go forward, you can go further than you ever dreamt.

The quote below neatly summarises how I understand the human being, a paradox of consistency and constant growth, so I share it with you in parting.

'A person is an active being who is perpetually engaged in becoming and yet remains identical with himself.'[142]

On our journey we are constantly moving forward, learning and being transformed, yet not changing who we are in a fundamental way. On the contrary, we are becoming more our true selves, more of who God always intended us to be.

That is what I wish for you: that you will be ever growing and at the same time always remain who you are at your core. I wish you all the best as you continue on your way. Remember all you have learnt, know that you are never alone, and take it one day at a time.

Wishing you much joy, strength and courage for your onward journey...

Belinda

---

[142] Boman, *Hebrew Thought Compared with Greek*, 49.

List of Emotions[145]

absorbed
abusive
accepting
accommodating
accomplished
adaptable
adversarial
aggressive
agreeable
alert
altruistic
analytical
angry
annoyed
antagonistic
anxious
approved of
arrogant
ashamed
authentic
balanced
beautiful
belligerent
bereft
bitter
bored
brave
broken down
bullied
calm
chaotic
cheerful
cold

commanding
compassionate
competitive
complaining
conceited
condemned
confident
conflicted
confused
conservative
content
controlled
controlling
cooperative
courageous
cowardly
creative
critical
cruel
curious
defeated
deluded
demanding
dependent
depressed
desperate
destitute
destructive
detached
dignified
disconnected
discouraged
disgusted

dominated
dominating
eccentric
ecstatic
egocentric
egotistical
empathic
empowered
envious
erratic
excited
expressive
extroverted
fair
faithful
fearful
frightened
frustrated
glad
good
grateful
greedy
grieving
guilty
happy
harmonising
hatred
helpful
helpless
hesitant
hopeless
idealistic
ignorant

[145] (http://www.higherawareness.com/self-healing/emotions-and-feelings.html)

impatient	moral	sad
important	negative	sadistic
impoverished	noble	secretive
impulsive	obsessed	self-accepting
in service	open	self-condemning
indifferent	panicked	self-defeating
individualistic	paranoid	self-destructive
inert	passionate	self-hatred
insecure	passive	selfish
insensitive	peaceful	self-obsessed
inspired	perfectionist	self-pity
interested	pitiful	self-sabotaging
intolerant	pleased	sensitive
introspective	poor	serene
invulnerable	possessive	shamed
irresponsible	powerful	shut-down
irritated	practical	shy
isolated	preoccupied	sorry
jealous	procrastinating	stable
joyful	proud	stimulated
judged	punished	stricken
judgmental	punishing	strung-out
lazy	purposeful	stubborn
likeable	rage	superior
lively	reactionary	tantrums
lonely	reclusive	timid
lost	rejected	tolerant
loved	rejoicing	unconcerned
loving	repressed	understanding
mad	resentful	unforgiving
manipulated	resigned	unhappy
manipulative	resistant	unresponsive
mediating	responsible	untrusting
miserable	ridiculous	vain
mistrusting	righteous	vengeance
moody	ruthless	vicious

victimized
violent
visionary
well-meaning
wise
withdrawn
worthy

Printed in the United States
By Bookmasters